TRAINING

for Results

Teaching
adults to be
independent,
assertive
learners

Bob Mosher,
with Lesley Darling and Ellen Fike

Cover: Design by Lauralee Haefner. Illustration by Sue Kochan. Interior: Layout and figures by Matt Fineout. Editors: Dana Luther and Peter Bauer.

ISBN 1-889176-00-1

Printed in the U. S. A.

Table of Contents

Preface

Our organization is a computer training center. As such, we offer training for adults who want to learn about a specific hardware or software. We provide trainer development for our on-site trainers, and for client trainers throughout the world. And we write and publish our own classroom materials, which are tested in our training center every day.

We have enjoyed much success with our style of training, and we'd like to share that success with you. In this book, you'll find tips and tools for successful training events, based on our experience over the years. You'll learn how to design and prepare effective training events. You'll learn how to change a dependent, passive training event into an independent, learner-focused training event. And you'll have the added benefit of learning our techniques, as well as the educational methodology behind our style.

Although this book was written with computer trainers in mind, you can adapt most of its topics to any type of training that involves adult learners. We believe that new trainers and veteran trainers alike will find this book useful.

We hope you enjoy the book and use it often. And we hope you'll take the challenge we offer to give adult learners responsibility for their own learning. Happy reading, and may you enjoy many exciting training events!

Introduction

Traditional training is instructor-led. The trainer is in charge of the learning that takes place. But research tells us that adults prefer to take responsibility for their own learning. In this book, we share some exciting ways to give adult learners the opportunity to take responsibility for their own learning. And we challenge you, the trainer, to loosen the reins of control.

As a trainer, your approach to each training event should be one of excitement about the information you are delivering. Keep in mind that there is at least one new idea that you can learn from each person in each of your training events. Encourage learners to share their ideas and experiences to help others. Create a classroom that is open, active, and learner directed. And don't be afraid to show your excitement and desire to learn; it motivates the people in your training event. One of the greatest compliments we receive in our classrooms is that our trainers are so energized and excited about their work. This style of learning is challenging and refreshing for both trainers and learners.

The order of the chapters in this book reflects the order in which we believe you will use the information. We begin by discussing adult learning as it differs from traditional or youth learning. Because adult learning is the basis for our approach to training, and because some trainers might not have a background in adult learning theory, we believe it is the best place to start. After a light dose of theory, we share our approach to training adult learners. How do we know our approach works? We use it successfully in our classrooms every day. And you can benefit from our experience.

A needs assessment is the first step in defining direction. It tells you where you are going. Effective solutions are based on the proper identification of problems. What do the learners need and want? If you decide that training is the solution, what specific needs will the training satisfy? Do the learners need to prepare for new jobs? Do they need to be more productive? Or do they want to pursue a new career? Needs are personal. Solutions are responses that meet those needs.

Once you know what the learners need, you can prescribe an appropriate solution. If training is the solution, you need to identify the type of training. Then list the tasks that learners need to demonstrate in order to satisfy their needs. These are your objectives. They determine how you will get where you are going.

Next you need to prepare for the training. This includes preparing yourself instructionally and physically, as well as preparing the setup for the classroom. The arrangement of the classroom and the tone of your voice can affect the training. Your teaching style and each person's learning style are important for the success of the training event. Be ready to change your style and pace as needed. Know and understand your subject matter and use more than one technique to present difficult topics. And practice channeling your anxiety in positive directions.

Concepts and procedures are often confused with one another. Concepts are ideas that enable understanding and learning. Procedures are logical steps based on concepts. When you teach concepts, learners relate the new information to familiar information. This way, they can relate their learning to their needs. Adult learners accept responsibility for learning if they believe it is relevant and relates to their needs.

Classroom management skills are rarely needed with adult learners. But if a behavior problem occurs, you should be ready to handle it and avoid further problems. Mismanagement of a situation can result in additional problems that threaten the success of your training event.

Evaluation is critical. It determines your direction and that of the learners as well. If the training event meets the needs of the learners, what is the next step? If the training event does not meet the needs of the learners, begin again with a needs assessment. Perhaps you incorrectly identified the problem. Or perhaps you misunderstood the circumstances. You need to know how to proceed before you can identify where you are

Training For Results

going. Additionally, evaluation helps you grow as a trainer. How well
are you doing? What areas do you need to work on? The more feedback
you get, the better you become.

After you experience a few training events using our approach, you
should feel excited about your work. To make sure that your excitement
continues, pay close attention to your stress level. A little bit of stress
keeps you motivated and challenged. But too much stress is dangerous.
You want to continue to enjoy your job and feel excited about each
training event. And you want to be the best trainer you can be.

About the authors

Bob Mosher is Manager of Product Research for Logical Operations, the largest publisher of computer applications training materials in the world. For years he has been involved in Trainer Development. He participates in employee instructor development as well as the development of client site instructors throughout the world. It is not out of the ordinary to see Bob in the classroom training people in Macintosh or DOS applications. For the last two years, he has been a faculty member for SOFTBANK Institute's Computer Training and Support Conference, teaching both pre-conference seminars and sessions on instructor development. Bob has eight years' experience as a computer trainer and instructor development specialist, five years as a public school teacher in computer science, and a masters degree in computer education.

Lesley Darling is the Director of Trainer Development at Logical Operations. She is responsible for employee instructor development as well as the development of client site instructors throughout the world. For the last three years she has been a faculty member for SOFTBANK Institute's Computer Training and Support Conference, and directed the trainer feedback theater. Lesley has four years' experience as a certified NetWare instructor and two years' experience in end-user training and employee development. Lesley has a bachelor's degree in communication studies.

Ellen Fike is a Technical Editor and Creative Writer for Logical Operations. In this book, she shares her research and studies in the areas of adult learning and trainer development, as well as proven tips and tools from the Logical Operations classrooms. Ellen is a certified public school teacher and has worked in areas of educational television and instructional design. In her previous role as Manager of Instructional Products at Logical Operations, she monitored the design and delivery of instructor products. Ellen has a bachelor's degree in English, teacher certification in secondary English and elementary education, and a master's degree in organizational communication.

The Complexity of Adult Learning

To stop learning is to stop growing. As a trainer, be eager to learn from each and every class you conduct. You will forever bloom.

Adult Learners and Change

What makes adult learners different from other learners? Adult learners are problem-centered and results-oriented. They are self-directed and not dependent on others. When adults experience a problem—a gap between where they are and where they want to be—they take steps to close the gap. In contrast, youths are subject-centered and future-oriented. They depend on adults for their direction. Unlike adult education, youth education is mandatory and designed for experimental purposes, all towards determining a future. Most of the subjects youths study are predetermined, leaving little or no choice for the youth. Whether or not the teacher is effective, youths must successfully complete each subject.

Adults approach learning with specific results in mind. They know where they want to be. Since adult education is mostly voluntary, adults tend to avoid or drop out of education that is not producing the results they seek. This means that training must be effective from beginning to end. Chapter 8, "Evaluation: Effective Training and Trainers," includes guidelines that you can use to check the effectiveness of your training.

Because adult learning often stems from problems, trainers must be more person-oriented than subject-oriented. Your training should be designed to help individuals cope with problems they are experiencing and attain their goals. For example, adult learners are more likely to attend a workshop on *Creating A Custom Spreadsheet* than a workshop on *Advanced Spreadsheet Principles*. The title *Creating A Custom Spreadsheet* clearly describes what the learners will be doing in the workshop. *Advanced Spreadsheet Principles* suggests that they will most likely be wading through theory. Adult learners will choose a clear, direct path to the results they want.

Keep in mind that all learning involves change—and change can be frightening and painful. Be sensitive to the individual needs of learners. They might be excited about learning new information and, at the same time, fearful because it involves a new career and uncertainties. Or they might be faced with changes in their present jobs that require new learning. Regardless of their reasons for attending training, they are all depending on you to help them succeed.

The Three Rs of Adult Learning

Adults master new information quickly when they have reason to believe that they can use the information to solve problems. Suppose you are about to begin a training session called *Creating A Custom Spreadsheet*. Before you can successfully teach adults how to create a spreadsheet, you need to tell them why they should learn this new concept and how they will benefit from its features. Explain which tasks they can perform better with this new information. Often an analogy is helpful. For example, to convey the benefits of replacing paper spreadsheets with electronic spreadsheets, explain that both types of spreadsheets have the same information. However, the electronic spreadsheet can be changed easily, and it updates automatically—no more erasing. If adult learners believe there is value in the learning, they will immediately relate this new information to the tasks in their jobs.

Adult learners decide whether or not to accept new information based on the three Rs: Relevancy, Relationship, and Responsibility. If the information is not timely, appropriate, and relevant to the learner's needs, he or she will not accept responsibility for the learning; the new information will be rejected. It is important to understand that you cannot make a learner accept new information. However, you can guide the learner toward a good decision.

1. Relevancy: Adults seek training that is timely and appropriate.

2. Relationship: Adults seek training that relates to their needs.

3. Responsibility: Adults accept responsibility for their own learning.

To increase the value of your training events, help learners find relevancy in the new information by pointing out accurate and meaningful relationships between new information and the learners' previous knowledge.

The presentation of information in this book to you, an adult learner, is based on the premise of the three Rs. As adult learners, you will decide whether or not to accept the responsibility of learning this information based on its relevancy and relationship to your needs and expectations. Analogies, examples, metaphors, and scenarios are some of the techniques that help you relate the new information to information that is already familiar to you.

Suppose your organization is changing its recordkeeping methods from paper forms to electronic forms. You've heard people talking about databases, but you don't know what a database is or how to use one. In fact, you don't even know what a database looks like. When you attend database training, the trainer begins class by holding up a telephone book. You quickly learn that the telephone book is an example of a database. After a discussion of how the names, addresses, and telephone numbers are easy to use in this format, the group defines a database as a set of related information. Then the trainer asks for other examples of databases. You learn that you already use several paper databases in your job and at home, and that an electronic database will simplify your tasks and help you become more efficient. Now you know what the new concept is, why you need to know about it, and how it can help you in your job. Having satisfied your quest for relevancy and relationship, you are ready to accept responsibility.

Adults are generally skeptical about new information, so they like to try it out before accepting it. This is why you need to engage learners in prompt hands-on events and practice as an essential component of the learning process. Let them experiment and test the new information on other situations that they are curious about. This demonstrates their understanding of the concept. By experimenting, they are working to relate the new information to other situations, which is the level of transfer you want them to achieve.

Thinking Styles

From the early stages of youth, people begin to develop a thinking style. Generally, they tend to use one of four styles: reflective, conceptual, practical, or creative. Although most people are capable of changing their thinking style to meet the situation at hand, they generally prefer one style in particular. When people learn, they prefer to receive information in a way that is familiar and suits their thinking style.

Every learner presents different challenges. And so it should be; after all, each person is a unique individual with particular needs and styles. To help you meet the needs and anticipate the thoughts of adult learners, you should first examine the characteristics of each style.

- *Reflective thinkers* view information subjectively, relating the new information to past experiences. They examine their feelings about what they are learning or doing. Reflective thinkers often ask "Why?" and they like to be actively involved in their learning. They might ask, "Why do I need to learn about charts? I don't ever use them!"

- *Conceptual thinkers* need to see the big picture before they can accept new information. They want to know the mechanics of how things work, not just see the outcome. They learn the concepts you present, and then want to know about concepts you might have left out.

- *Practical thinkers* want factual information without the fluff of additional, nice-to-know information. They try to find the simplest, most effective way to perform their work successfully. Practical thinkers are not satisfied until they know how to apply their new skills to their job.

- *Creative thinkers* like to tinker with new information. They are always asking "Why?" and will work tirelessly to find answers to present and potential problems. This makes them excellent troubleshooters. They create their own shortcuts, and often try to take a computer application far beyond its intended use.

When you consider your teaching style, also consider the learners' thinking styles. If individual learners are having difficulty with any concepts, try varying your teaching style to match their thinking style.

Brain Dominance

"Brain dominance" refers to your natural tendency to think and act according to the characteristics of one side of your brain versus the other side. The left side of your brain determines your ability to be disciplined, perform logical deductions, and use language, writing, and mathematics.

The right side of your brain affects your imagination and your artistic and intuitive abilities. When a person suffers a stroke that damages the left side of the brain, he or she might have difficulty formulating thoughts and physically speaking. Damage to the right side of the brain might cause a person to suffer a loss of artistic ability, but not speech.

Although some abilities are specific to one side of the brain, other abilities require the cooperation of both left and right sides. Nerve fibers connect the left and right sides of the brain, allowing messages to pass between the two. This enables you to perform tasks that require abilities from both sides, such as conducting a training event, in which you need to use language and create scenarios to explain new concepts.

Most people develop a preference for using one side of the brain over the other. They are identified as left-brained and right-brained according to their tendencies. The more you use the preferred side, the better your performance becomes. And since you tend to use the preferred side most often, the other side becomes less efficient. This is similar to using the mouse with your dominant hand. After an extended period of time, try using the mouse with your other hand. It feels clumsy and uncoordinated. But with practice, you can become proficient with both hands.

See if you can identify your tendencies in the table.

Left-Brain Preferences	Right-Brain Preferences
Rules, processes, and systems	Flexibility
Perform one task at a time	Multi-tasking
Order	Change and challenge
Neat and organized	Bright colors
Serious, factual, logical	Tight schedules
Attention to detail	Look for the "big picture"

You might immediately identify yourself as left-brained or right-brained, but the people you work with might identify you as the opposite style. This could simply mean that you act differently at work than you act at home. This is common, because you are naturally more comfortable in your own environment.

According to your tendencies, is your profession in line with your style?

Common Professions of Left-Brained People	Common Professions of Right-Brained People
Accountant	Entertainer
Researcher	Teacher
Computer Technician	Writer
Scientist	Counselor
Engineer	Speaker
Banker	Salesperson

Although tendencies affect chosen professions, there are exceptions. Suppose that at work you are perceived as an outgoing person, and as a result, you land a sales position. It's a great job, yet you're not happy. You don't enjoy meeting the clients and attending conventions. In fact, social gatherings of any type are draining experiences for you. And this makes your job exhausting and unfulfilling. Outside of work, you shy away from social events. You go home on Friday and stay close to home until Monday morning when you go off to work again. And after a vacation, it is difficult for you to build up energy for your first day back on the job. Your outgoing personality at work might be a disguise for your nervousness around people.

Many people have a tendency to be left-brained in some situations and right-brained in other situations. This might mean that you are aware of your tendencies, but you are also working to develop your weaker side.

But on the other hand, it might mean that the two sides are in conflict. You might be favoring your tendencies and denying your other side. Even though you have tendencies toward one side of the brain, you will be more efficient if you also develop the other side. For example, the left side and the right side of the brain each have strengths. By using both sides together, you might assume that you double your strengths. In reality, you more than double your strengths because you can now accomplish tasks that require characteristics of both sides of the brain. The key is to work with your natural tendency because it yields the most energy, and at the same time respect and develop the other side of your brain. Your goal is to become whole-brained, using both sides of your brain in harmony.

Key Learning Styles

Learning styles are similar to working and thinking styles. Most people tend to be predominantly one type of learner. That is not to say that each learner can learn only when new information is presented in their particular style. Even though learners have preferred styles, they can often adapt to another style. The style that a learner prefers is determined by the style that is used when the learner experiences success. The learner tends to look for that particular style in each learning experience. When you have multiple learning styles in one setting, you need to vary your style throughout the training session to accommodate all types of learners.

- The *auditory learner* processes new information best when the information is spoken. A lecture is a successful technique. You might not need to use any props or aids to help auditory learners make the connection between the information you are speaking and the way learners will use the information. Auditory learners might make the connection as quickly as you speak.

- The *visual learner* processes new information best when the information is demonstrated or illustrated. Instructor demonstrations, role playing, and drawing pictures are successful techniques. For example, to explain how memory works in a computer, you might want to draw a measuring cup on the board. Then draw a line to show how much memory is used. Explain that each time you save more information, the line goes up until the cup is full. Then you can discuss the need for more memory.

- The *kinesthetic learner* processes new information best when the information can be touched or manipulated. Keying the steps to create something, taking notes, examining items, and participating in activities are successful techniques. For example, to help kinesthetic learners understand the parts of a computer and how the unit works, you and the learners can take apart a computer and have learners examine the parts.

- The *environmental learner* processes new information best when the surroundings are adjusted to fit his or her liking (room temperature, lighting, noise level, room arrangement, and so on). Develop a climate that helps people feel comfortable and ready to learn. You might have to adjust settings often during the training session to accommodate everyone. (But not so much that the adjustment becomes disruptive or impedes learning!)

Key Learning Elements

Active involvement in the learning process energizes adults, both as participants and designers of their learning. They bring knowledge, experience, and attitudes about learning to the classroom. Remember, they already know why they chose this training: they want to use it to fill the gap between where they are and where they want to be. By asking preliminary questions, you can identify a learner's skills. Then, be sure to acknowledge those skills. And reassure learners that, just as they will be learning from you and others in the class, you will be learning from them.

Adults prefer to solve problems rather than to be given solutions. This is because they want to be responsible for their own learning, not to be dependent on you. To challenge learners, create problems that they can solve in the learning environment. For example, to help people understand how to change the font of text, you might begin by showing them how to change the font of one letter. Then tell them to change the font of an entire paragraph. Rather than change the font one letter at a time, they will most likely experiment until they find a way to change the font of the entire paragraph at once.

Training should address specific needs. Adults relate new information to familiar information and then ask questions that help them find solutions to specific problems they've encountered. Therefore, you should come to class prepared with scenarios and personal experiences that learners can use to practice on during class.

Training should be job-related. Use scenarios and examples that relate to the learner's job. You want the learner to be able to return to his or her job and immediately apply the learning.

Chapter Two

A Logical Approach to Training

Give the learner responsibility for learning and you will turn passive, dependent learners into assertive, independent learners.

Traditional training is instructor-led. The trainer is in charge of the learning that takes place. Therefore, the responsibility for learning is on the trainer, not on the learner. The learner is passive and dependent on the trainer for information and direction. This puts a burden on the trainer to make sure the learner learns. *You can lead a horse to water, but you can't make him drink.* And based on our findings in Chapter 1, "The Complexity of Adult Learning," adult learners prefer to be responsible for their own learning. They want to take charge of their lives, not sit passively, dependent on the trainer. Yet according to trainers, instructor-led training is the most popular style of training today. This can be attributed to several factors:

- Instructor-led training is easier for the trainer because there is minimal risk. Instructor-led training implies that the trainer is in control of the training event at all times.

- Change is risky. Your credibility as a trainer is at stake.

- Training is designed by trainers, not learners. So it meets the needs of trainers, not learners.

- It's always been that way.

Yet, as trainers, we claim that our role is to meet the needs of learners, so what are we doing to support that claim? Trainers everywhere need to relinquish the reins of control and help learners accept responsibility for their own learning. It isn't an easy task; in fact, it's risky. But if we don't do it, we can't meet the needs of learners.

As we stated earlier, the traditional classroom creates dependent, passive learners. It does not create independent learners who are responsible for their own learning. Adults come to training fully expecting to be *told* new information, and they expect by the end of the training event to know everything because they've been *told* everything. Nowhere in their plans are thoughts of participating or interacting in training. Yet, by nature, adults prefer to participate in their learning.

This chapter explains why the traditional classroom creates dependent, passive learners. And it shows you how to create independent learners who eagerly accept responsibility for learning. Best of all, we know this approach works because we use it successfully in our classrooms every day. It's a refreshing new style of learning welcomed by both trainers and learners. Like teaching Johnny to ride a bicycle, there's a certain excitement and satisfaction for both you and Johnny when he decides he wants to ride his bicycle without training wheels and without you holding on.

Traditional Training versus Independent Learning

Let's look at the areas of support for training. Have you ever taken a course only to get back to the office and have problems with the software or with something you learned in class? Who did you call for help?

Probably the trainer or the Help Desk for that particular training. Help Desks were created to replace the trainer after the training event; they help learners after the class is completed. If you can't reach the trainer or the Help Desk for answers, your next choice is probably a peer, or another person who was in the training event. If a peer is not available, learners tend to reach for the courseware, or manual, from the training class. The on-line Help system is generally the last resort.

Traditional Training versus Independent Learning

Traditional Training	Independent Learning
Trainer/Help Desk	On-line Help system
Peer	Courseware and user's guides
Courseware and user's guides	Peer
On-line Help system	Trainer/Help Desk

The table above, Traditional Training versus Independent Learning, compares the priority of support levels for each style. Notice that the difference between numbers 1 and 2, and numbers 3 and 4 on both sides of the table illustrates the difference between dependent learning and independent learning. The Trainer/Help Desk and the peer represent dependent learning because the learner depends on another person. The on-line Help system and the courseware and user's guides represent independent learning because the learner depends only on him- or herself to find answers, not on others.

Independent learning helps people solve their own problems. It challenges trainers to put themselves and the Help Desk at the bottom of the list for support (number 4 in the table instead of number 1). Independent learners want to solve their own problems, rather than ask you to solve them. And this is what you should encourage them to do.

In the past, on-line Help systems were poorly designed; people complained that they were useless. But today's on-line Help systems are much improved—so much so that we've elevated them to number 1 in the area of support. If you are training people to use a software that has a poor on-line Help system, or you are teaching a topic that does not include an on-line Help system, you might need to move the on-line Help system to a lower priority to fit your particular needs. But you should never move the trainer and the Help Desk back to number 1. Independent learning requires the trainer and the Help Desk to be the last resort for support.

If you expect people to use their manuals for support and reference, don't overlook the importance of choosing top-quality courseware. When you evaluate courseware, check the topics in the manual. Are they the same topics you need to teach? Are the concepts clearly written and easy to understand, yet rich with information? The flow and readability of the information in the manual are important for continuity and understanding. The manual must be useful as a reference after class as well as during class.

Fears

As a trainer, you need to create a comfortable atmosphere when people approach the classroom. Put on a smile, turn up the lights, and use a friendly tone to welcome people to the room. And write the name of the training event on the board or flip chart ahead of time to help learners eliminate one of their fears—that they are in the wrong place.

Typically, adults become set in their ways as they grow older. They often resist change because it threatens their familiar settings. Think about your lifestyle in particular—you've probably established a network of friends, co-workers, and associates. You've even arranged your home and work area in a way that makes you feel comfortable. And of course you have your own way of getting things done. So when someone suddenly says, "We're changing things. You'll have to learn new ways," you experience fear. This may happen even when you know that change can bring new challenge and positive results. You want to protect your empire of familiar places, faces, and work habits. Have you ever heard people complain again and again about something, and still not take action to change it? Sometimes the benefits of growth aren't considered with the risks.

In addition to fearing personal changes, learners fear the training location because it is different from the work location. As soon as learners arrive, they begin looking for something familiar. Adults expect to see a traditional classroom setup. And they feel a certain amount of comfort and ease when they do see it. We all feel more comfortable in a familiar setting, even if it isn't the best setting. Although the traditional classroom setup comes out of the old passive tradition, your event won't be passive. And you will be starting with something nonthreatening.

Adults have responsibilities outside the training event as well as inside. They worry about emergencies at home and at the office. What if others need to reach them right away? You will be able to hold their attention much easier if you address these issues early. Before you begin class, write the schedule on the board. List lunch and break times as well as start and finish times. At the beginning of class, discuss the schedule and let people know if your schedule is flexible. Tell them where they can find the rest rooms, telephones, and refreshments. Also explain that someone will be taking calls and messages for them. If an emergency arises, they will be contacted right away.

Adults have fears that most trainers never address. These include the classroom equipment, other people in the class, the seating arrangement, and you, the trainer. Let people know that they can sit anywhere, and then explain your style of teaching. Tell people that this is not a traditional training event in which they must sit quietly and raise their hands before speaking. Learners should feel comfortable talking to one another during problem-solving activities and discussions. To help people learn to use their peers effectively, encourage them to get to know the person sitting next to them and others in the class, and to share ideas and questions. Throughout the day, people might want to exchange work telephone numbers, experiences, or business cards if they work at different locations. Explain that they should be supporting each other when they return to their respective workplaces. If the learners are all from the same company, they will be working together after the class.

Learners may have the opportunity to reconvene, but the trainer moves on to another class or another training site. If learners try to contact the trainer after class to solve a problem, they might have to wait until the trainer can call them back. Most trainers have several training events each week, so the trainer might not remember the learner right away. And it probably takes the person at the Help Desk at least half the total telephone time to learn the job-related information the peer in the next cubicle already knows. Peers are close by and already familiar with the situation and the workplace.

Responsibility for Learning

Before you can transfer the responsibility for learning to the learners, you need to tell them what you are doing. Remember that they are expecting a traditional training style, not a progressive style. You need to help them understand how you intend to accomplish this transfer. And you need to make it happen without interfering with valuable training time. Begin by explaining that you will not be instructing; instead, you'll be *facilitating* discussion. The training will be more effective if everyone participates in the discussions, so be sure to consider their contributions equally.

You'll also want to let people know how you intend to handle questions. Encourage questions and explain that all questions are good questions. Suggest that even though one person asks a question, more than one person will be interested in the answer. And often, one question leads to another, which might resolve other problems. To encourage questions, try using the *parking lot* technique. On the board or flip chart, draw a large box with lines to resemble a parking lot. When someone asks a question that you want to defer to a more appropriate time, write the question in abbreviated form inside the parking lot. If the question concerns a topic covered in another chapter or lesson in the course, write the number of the chapter or lesson next to the question. If the question concerns a topic not covered in the course, write "break" or "after class" next to the question. As each chapter or lesson ends, check the parking lot to see if there are any questions still to be answered. Tell the people in your class to remind you if you miss a question. This technique assures learners that their questions will be answered.

At the beginning of the training event, introduce yourself and the people in your class. The sooner learners get to know each other, the sooner they can begin sharing information and experiences. Include your name, your experience in the subject area you are teaching, your job, and what you expect to get out of this training event. Judging from the size of the class and the skill levels of the learners, you can give either a short or long introduction. For a group of advanced learners, you might want to encourage introductions that give additional information, such as education and hobbies. For introductory-level learners, you might need to conserve time for later. When you introduce yourself, model the type and detail of information you want others to provide.

You'll notice we've started small by giving learners responsibility in stages. Already they know that they will be participating in discussions, monitoring questions, and possibly controlling the schedule for the day. The reason for transferring responsibility in stages is to avoid overwhelming the learners. Remember, they aren't used to this style of learning. It isn't that they can't handle responsibility, but instead that the opportunity is new to them.

Once learners know that they are allowed to take charge, they will eagerly accept more responsibility during the course of the training event. As the day goes on, the roles of the trainer and learners will begin to trade involvement levels. The trainer becomes less involved as the learners become more involved. You'll notice people initiating discussions, and asking each other questions rather than asking you. Don't be afraid to let this happen. In fact, you should encourage this kind of participation. This learning support system is called the *ramp down, ramp up* model. The training event begins with high trainer involvement and low learner involvement. By the end of the training event, trainer involvement is low and learner involvement is high. This model strengthens classroom learning by connecting the learning to the industry with the effect of on-the-job training. And when people return to the workplace, they find that they can hit the ground running, which is often just what their organizations expect. Learners are simply transferring their new skills to specific situations in their workplaces.

The Blob

Before people can take charge of their learning, you need to provide them with the necessary tools. It's not enough to tell them that they will be responsible for their own learning. You need to tell them how you intend to work with them and accomplish the transfer of responsibility from trainer to learner. Each person comes to training with a specific set of expectations called their "blob." In an ideal setting, you would deliver a customized training event for each learner. But because the training that you provide must meet everyone's needs, it includes topics that some people don't want or need. When you present the list of topics that you will be covering in class (your blob), you will be providing more than enough for each person. Each person's blob is affected by motivation, ability, and need. Even though you promise a large blob of information, each learner will receive only the information that he or she is motivated to receive, is able to use, and has a need to know.

As the term implies, a visual representation of the information you will present, along with each learner's motivation, ability, and need looks like a blob. As you explain how you will conduct the training event, illustrate your message. This helps visual learners as well as auditory learners. Draw a large irregular shape. Explain that the shape, or "blob," represents all the information that will be presented in the training event. For example, if this is an introductory word processing course, the basic blob will contain information such as inserting and deleting text, scrolling a document, formatting, mail merge, saving a document, copying and pasting, and spell checking.

Because each person's motivation, ability, and need is different, his or her expectations also will be different. For example, suppose Bob needs to learn how to create documents. To illustrate Bob's blob, draw a smaller blob inside the large drawing (because creating documents is included in this course). Perhaps Sally needs to learn how to create documents, and she needs to learn mail merge. Draw Sally's blob inside your blob with a small amount overlapping Bob's blob: Sally's needs also are included in the course, and like Bob, Sally needs to learn to create documents. Jane already knows how to create documents and do mail merge. She needs to learn how to create professional reports and insert graphs from other software packages. Draw Jane's blob outside your blob with a small amount extending inside. Her needs do not match most of the topics taught in this course. The drawing shows that this training offers very little new information for Jane. Maybe she's in the wrong class, or maybe this is a refresher course for her. As the trainer, you want to meet everyone's needs. But remember to focus on the course objectives. As we discussed earlier, you might be able to attend to some of Jane's questions during breaks or after class.

The Blob

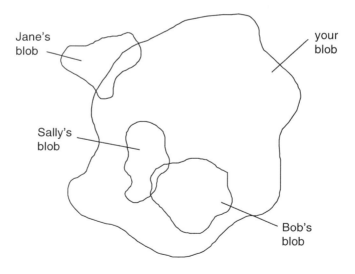

Use the drawing to help you explain why you need to present all of the information in the blob. The learner is responsible for only the information he or she needs or wants. Tell people that when you are teaching information that they don't need or want, they can either sit quietly so others who need this information can learn, or they can participate because they might need or want this information later. Learners should not expect everything in the course to pertain to only their personal needs. Ask people to be patient because you will be discussing their topics, too.

Design Models

Tell them what you're going to tell them.

Tell them.

Tell them what you told them.

You've probably heard this old paradigm, the Tell Them Model, used many times. It is a good approach for mapping content and designing training. But it is not a good approach for the delivery of training. Here's why. When you use this model, who is responsible for learning? The trainer is *telling* the learner, which indicates one-way communication. Nowhere does the learner accept any responsibility. In fact, the learner might not even participate other than listening.

The Setup/Delivery/Follow-up (SDF) Model goes hand in hand with the Tell Them Model to create a sound design for training. But too many trainers make the mistake of also using these models to deliver the training. Here's why that won't work. When you introduce a new topic, you bridge the new material to familiar material, and you explain why the information is useful. You, the trainer, are in control of the setup. That doesn't necessarily mean that you are doing all of the talking. You might just lead or direct a discussion. Your style of delivering the information might be one of mutual control between you and the learners. Perhaps learners will be participating in discussion or discovery learning. Or you might have learners perform a hands-on activity. Follow-up involves testing comprehension. And this is where most trainers test *procedures* when they should be testing *concepts*.

The follow-up that you use determines whether you are testing procedures or concepts, and whether the learning is dependent or independent. If you use questions such as "How do you copy a paragraph to another document?", you are testing for the copy procedure. The answer to this question requires the learner to list the steps of the procedure. It is a memorization test. It doesn't prove that the learner knows why copying text is important or how to apply the skill to other situations. If you use a follow-up statement such as "In summary, we learned how to copy text from one document and paste it into another document," you are testing your own memorization of the copy procedure. Learners haven't done anything except perhaps nod their heads. Notice how this fits with "Tell them what you're going to tell them, tell them, and tell them what you told them." Questions such as "Why would we want to copy this paragraph to another document?" and "What specific things can you use the Copy command for back at your workplace?" test for concepts. The answer is not a list of procedures. In fact, the procedures aren't important. They're in the book, available to be looked up anytime. These questions require an explanation of the concept. Learners must understand the concept and be able to apply it to other situations.

Setup/Delivery/Follow-up Model (SDF)

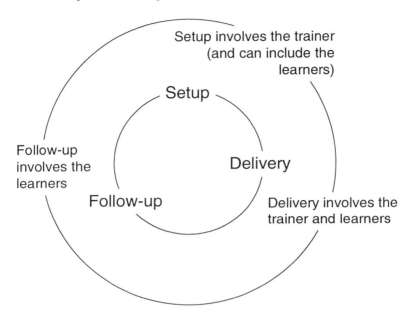

Use the drawing of the Setup/Delivery/Follow-up (SDF) Model to determine whether you are testing for procedures or concepts. The inner circle illustrates the setup, delivery, follow-up process. The outer circle illustrates the level of involvement in each part of the process. During the setup, the trainer is involved. And learners might also be involved. You might provide a storyline or an analogy, or you might lead a discussion. The delivery involves both the trainer and the learners. In follow-up, the key is to test learners for concepts, not procedures. Learners might perform a hands-on activity or participate in a discussion. When you present a follow-up activity, who is performing the activity? If you are demonstrating the activity, you are testing yourself. If you ask how to do something, you are testing for procedures. But you want the learners to perform. If you ask questions in the follow-up, what types of answers are required? Your questions should require people to relate the information they are learning to other situations. Remember: if you are doing the follow-up and the learners aren't participating, you are testing for procedures. And you are using the Tell Them Model.

A comparison of the Traditional Training Model and the Independent Learning Model shows the difference between the two styles. The Traditional Training Model follows the SDF and Tell Them Models exactly. The trainer accomplishes his or her objectives of delivering the information. But there is no evidence that learners learn the information. In the Independent Learning Model, the trainer uses techniques that require learners to demonstrate learning and meet their personal needs. Both the trainer and the learners accomplish their objectives.

The Traditional Training Model

Design Procedure	Purpose	Example of Delivery
Setup	Tell them what you're going to tell them.	This lesson covers procedures for copying and pasting text.
Delivery	Tell them.	To copy text, select the text, click on the Copy button, position the cursor where you want the copied text to appear, and click on the Paste button.
Follow-up	Tell them what you told them.	To summarize the Copy procedure: 1. Select the text you want to copy. 2. Click on the Copy button. 3. Position the cursor where you want the copied text to appear. 4. Click on the Paste button.

The Independent Learning Model

Design Procedure	Purpose	Example of Delivery
Setup	Present new information by using a storyline, analogy, discussion, or other method of interaction.	In what types of documents do you see the same text over and over again? Have you ever noticed that the text in most loan agreements is similar?
Delivery	Help learners try new ideas, perform hands-on activities, discuss experiences, or use problem-solving techniques to discover new information.	In the last lesson, we wrote a letter to the XYZ Company explaining our new product. We'd like to use some of the same text in other letters. How can we use the text again without typing it each time?
Follow-up	Help learners practice, brainstorm, or discuss ideas for situations that relate to the skills they are learning.	What types of tasks can you use the copy procedure for at your office? When would you find it more useful to move text instead of copying it?

Although your before-class tasks are accomplished separately from the training event, they are also important parts of an effective training model. If you prepare a lesson plan for your training events, you might want to include the tasks you perform before you begin the class.

- Arrive at the training location before the people in your class arrive.

- Prepare a comfortable, pleasing environment by turning on the lights, and by writing the name of the course, your name, and the schedule on the board or flip chart. When people arrive, put on a smile and welcome each person.

- Start the class with a formal welcome, and introduce yourself and the name of the course.

- Explain where the facilities are located (rest rooms, telephones, and refreshments).

- Explain how emergencies will be handled.

- Discuss the schedule and your flexibility regarding lunch and break times.

- Explain how you will handle questions (use the parking lot and blob techniques).

- Overview the course and the objectives.

- Model a detailed introduction and then ask learners to introduce themselves.

- Begin the course.

Chapter Three

Needs Assessment

If you don't know what you want, how will you know when you get it?

Which came first—the problem or the solution? The answer seems fairly obvious. Yet organizations commonly try to find solutions without ever identifying the problem. This leads to frustration and failed attempts to fix things. And this is why many training events are labeled ineffective. They didn't work because they weren't the right solution.

Adults are often perfectionists, eager to try to solve problems as quickly as possible. As such, they like to fix things and make them all nice and neat. And they often lose sleep if problems aren't fixed right away. Some organizations are the same way: they are made up of people who tend to jump to the conclusion that training is the answer to all problems. And when it doesn't solve the immediate problem, training is said to be ineffective. Yet it might not have been the right solution for the problem. Organizations and training consultants cannot identify the solution until they identify the problem, and that takes time and careful consideration.

How do you identify an organization's problem? And how do you prescribe a solution? A needs assessment is a tool that gets to the core of an organization's problems and identifies the needs of learners. The solution is based on the results of the assessment. But who conducts the needs assessment? Some training organizations offer up-front consultation and a needs assessment. Other training organizations expect client organizations to conduct their own needs assessments. In this case, the training organization is contacted only after the client organization has determined that training is the proper way to solve the problem. Depending on your situation, you might be responsible only for delivering the training event. Or you might be the salesperson and consultant, as well as the trainer. Whether or not you conduct your own needs assessments, you should understand how to conduct a needs assessment and how to use the results for a successful training event.

Training should be offered as an answer to a defined need, not a solution to all problems. The solution might include a combination of training, new or additional equipment, personnel intervention, and process change. Needs assessment begins in the beginning—the very beginning—long before training. And it continues beyond the training event. Before you spend valuable time developing training, you need to identify the problem. Then, if and when training is recommended, begin thinking about the type of training that is best for the situation at hand.

Assessing Needs Before Class

Suppose you are a manager for an organization. You purchased high-speed, high-tech computers last year, and a decision was made to change to a new software program. According to reports, you can't find anything to show that this purchase increased efficiency or productivity. You might be quick to assume the obvious—workers need training so they can use the computers and the new software to help them work efficiently. So you send everyone to a class to learn how to use the new computers and the software. After three months, you again look at the reports only to find that performance levels are the same. Now you've invested even more time and money, and you still have the same problem. Was the training ineffective? Did the trainer do a poor job?

Research, observation, or an informal interview with the workers would have revealed the real problem—the computers are on back order, and employee morale has plummeted to a record low due to recent changes.

Workers are still using their old computers and the old software. And they are afraid to share their frustrations with you. Valuable time and money have been wasted. Now you need to look into why the computers are still on back order, and then coordinate training efforts with the delivery of the new computers. Employees need assurance that you will work with them to alleviate their frustrations. Even if the first training event was excellent, adults process only information that they can use *now*. And they learn by practicing their new skills in real-world settings. Neither of these requirements is being met. You might think that this scenario can't happen, but it does, and it happens often.

Now that you understand why needs assessments are important, let's examine the three-step process of a needs assessment:

1. Identify the problem. Use special tools to get to the core of the problem. An important part of this is verifying that you have identified the *problem*, not just the symptoms.

2. Recommend a solution. Is training the answer? Who needs the training? Do the trainees agree that training is the answer? What types of training are needed? When should the training occur?

3. Evaluate the solution. Did you prescribe the right solution? What worked and what didn't work? What could have been better? What would you do differently next time?

A needs assessment involves an informal study of the organization. It reveals such information as specialized needs, personal opinions, company climate, and employee attitudes and morale. This information helps the organization make the right choice when selecting a solution.

In the previous scenario, the training solution was good, but it was not timely. Training should have been coordinated with the delivery of the equipment. That way, learners could have practiced and begun using their new skills right away. In the example organization, upon receipt of the new computers and software, the full training program will have to be implemented again. Before the second training, the organization should consider using needs-assessment tools. Some commonly used assessment tools are:

- Informal and formal interviews

- Questionnaires

- Surveys

- Research

- Observation

- Reports

- Advisory committees

Generally, informal methods are most effective. People like to help solve problems. Given a comfortable setting and informal techniques, people are more apt to "roll up their sleeves" and help because they believe they are part of the solution.

Before you decide what types of solutions to use, arrange to have learners fill out self-assessment forms. Often, you can order such forms from publishers. Or you can design your own forms. A good self-assessment tool should contain questions about experience, interests, and frustrations. Here are some sample self-assessment questions.

- What is your job title?

- What are the duties that you perform in your current job?

- What frustrates you in your current job?

- What new areas might interest you?

- Do you have any new ideas that you want to share?

Notice that these areas reveal needs, not skills. Based on the identified needs of the learner, a set of skills can be prescribed. You the trainer, not the learner, are the expert at identifying needs. And as such, you will want to follow the proper procedure. Ask questions that reveal the root of the need. Your assessment should be made up of three parts: identify the need, prescribe the solution, and then evaluate the solution. Valid assessment questions yield responses in the form of personal interests and ideas. For example, if you ask, "What do you need to learn to perform your job?", the learner's response will identify skills, and perhaps not appropriate skills. Instead, ask a question such as "What do you do in a typical work day?" Based on the learner's response, you can identify skills that will satisfy those needs. And you might be able to recommend a solution that the learner would not have otherwise received.

Assessing Needs During Class

In most cases, your work begins if and when training is identified as the solution to the problem. You might have to develop training from scratch or customize an existing training course. Or you might be teaching an off-the-shelf course. Regardless of the type of course, you will want to customize it somewhat to meet individual needs. By assessing the needs of the learners to find out their individual objectives, you can modify your style and the course. And you should continue to assess learners' needs throughout the training event. This allows you to maximize your presentation. You might find that you need to slow your pace or adjust your style to accommodate learners. Or you might need to pick up the pace. This is something you can adjust as many times during the event as you find necessary. Some topics are easier to understand than other topics, and some are easier for you to present than others. Constant monitoring of needs helps you stay in touch with the learners. You should not be surprised by anything you read on the evaluations of the training and your presentation. Instead, you should be aware of how each learner is receiving your presentation and the information throughout the training event.

Even if you, the trainer, are not personally conducting the formal needs assessment, there is always some level of assessment that a trainer can and should do. Your ongoing assessment might yield only small changes, but the results can be critical. For example, if you find that the data files and storylines used in the course are not helpful to the learners, you can make a small change that helps learners understand. By using analogies that relate to the learners' work situations, you can help learners use the data files successfully.

There are several ways you can assess the needs of learners during class.

- One of the first exercises you should do at any training event is introduce yourself and the people in your class. Starting with you, give your name, job title, experience with the software being taught in this class, and computer experience in general. When people share information, they learn from each other. They learn more than the information you are presenting. You'll also want to ask people to share their expectations for the class. This way, you might be able to adjust your teaching to include other areas in your goals for the event. And you can let people know if those expectations cannot be met in this course. Either way, you'll be aware of people's needs and expectations.

- During breaks, mingle with the people who are attending the training event. Ask questions about their background and interests. This is a relaxed time when people can share information naturally, without pressure. You might want to ask questions like, "Have you used the new software yet?", "What do you do in your job?", and "Are you excited about today's training event?"

- From time to time during class, check in with learners to make sure you are presenting the information clearly. Ask questions like, "Are you with me so far?", "Have any of you used this feature before?", "Since many of you expressed interest in this area in the beginning of class, do you want to spend more time on this topic?", and "Do you have any other questions before we move on?"

- Independent and group activities provide time for you to observe performance. Move around the room and observe the learners as they progress through activities. Listen to their discussions to find out if they are challenged or frustrated. You might also pick up some examples or topics that you should clarify with the group. Pay close attention to questions asked and answered by learners. These can indicate interests as well as frustration levels. You want to ensure that learners will be able to apply their new skills on the job when they return to their workplaces.

By assessing the needs of learners, you can determine the preferences of your target audience. This is important for your preparation as well as your delivery of information. Aim for the group that meets the requirements of the prerequisites. This is your target audience. Your style of teaching differs based on your target audience. For example, suppose your class is made up of 16 people: 3 advanced level, 2 novices lacking some of the prerequisites, and the rest meeting the prerequisites for the course. You need to challenge the advanced-level people and keep the novice learners from getting frustrated, and at the same time satisfy the middle group and meet the objectives for the course. Although this can be a difficult task, you can learn to do it well.

For example, if you find that you are finishing the class early, you might want to try to meet some individual needs of learners. You can present a scenario and ask learners to solve it using their new skills. Or you can add steps to a practice activity. Both ideas challenge the middle group and the advanced-level group. Then, while they are working on the activity, you can spend a few minutes working with the novice learners on the basic skills. But be sure you are meeting the objectives for the course before you try to meet additional needs. Remember, you are only one person, and you cannot address everyone's needs all the time.

Prerequisites help you identify the target audience. Ideally, you want every person who takes your course to succeed. But if you're going to lose anyone, from which group would you prefer to lose him or her? Suppose that, as you teach the course, you are trying to work individually with one of the novice learners. You practically teach the course from this learner's side. At the end of the course, you are very excited because you've helped the novice learner succeed in the course. What you didn't realize is that while you were spending additional time with the novice learner, you were alienating the learners in the middle group. You were so busy that you didn't notice the signs of frustration in the group. In fact, it was the evaluations after class that pointed out your mistake. Helping the novice learner succeed was noble of you, but you did it at the expense of other learners and your objectives. In this situation, you should talk to the novice learner about getting into the right class. Let him or her know that you are obligated to meet the objectives you agreed upon for this class. Stay focused on your target audience. Sometimes people simply get into the wrong class, and all you have to do is direct them to the right class. Other times, people insist on taking a course they aren't ready for. This is a situation that you might not be able to control. First and foremost, you are obligated to your target audience.

Assessing Needs After Class

After-class assessment is critical. Yet trainers often make the mistake of ending the training program as soon as the learners complete the training event. Just as training starts long before the training event, it continues long after the training event. The needs assessment is not complete until it has been determined whether or not the training was well received and successful. As the trainer, you are responsible for determining the learners' needs and delivering a successful training event based on those needs. Without an after-class assessment, you cannot determine if the learners' needs were met.

To conduct an after-class assessment, return to your before-class assessment tools (such as interview, questionnaire, survey, and observation). What were the needs of the learners? Were learners concerned about job changes? Did they hope to get a promotion? Were they trying to increase their productivity in order to keep their jobs? What did they hope to get out of this training? Did your objectives directly relate to the learners' needs? By answering these questions, you can determine your next step.

When learners' needs are met, behavioral changes occur. These changes are demonstrated in many ways, such as increased productivity, positive attitudes, high morale, and decrease in turnover. But if learners' needs are not met, the original problem will continue, and additional problems might surface. An investigation of the situation will reveal why the learners' needs were not met. Was the training ineffective? Was the trainer ineffective? Is the needs assessment valid?

Your after-class assessment should consist of the same list of needs the learners gave you before class. Ask learners if they are ready to apply for that promotion. Or ask them if they qualify for that new job. Did productivity increase? Further, you should ask these questions again in six months. How are they doing? If nothing has changed, the training might have been ineffective for some reason. Or maybe management did not buy into the training, and will not support the learner's new direction. The next step is to reassess the learners' needs, write new objectives, and redesign the training. Perhaps your first assessment incorrectly identified needs, or maybe your solution was incorrect. (See Kirkpatrick's Four Levels of Evaluation in Chapter 8, "Evaluation: Effective Training and Trainers.")

Objectives That Work

If you don't know where you are going, you can't get there from here.

Would you think of starting out on a trip to "Anytown" without first getting directions? Where is "Anytown"? Which way do you go—north, south, east, or west? The same holds true for training events. You need to know where you are going. Which way should you go? How do you get there? Objectives are tools that enable you to design, implement, and evaluate training. They describe where you are going and how you will get there. They identify skills that successful learners will be able to demonstrate by the end of the course. Without this information, you can't plan the training event. You can't explain what learners will do during the training. And you won't know what tasks to include in the manuals that learners will use. Objectives drive the training event.

By now you have conducted your needs assessment, and identified the learners' needs. The objectives you write are critical, and will focus directly on those needs.

Instructional Objectives vs. Behavioral Objectives

For every training event, you need to identify both instructional and behavioral (sometimes called performance) objectives. *Instructional objectives* include information and skills you need to teach learners so that they can accomplish the behavioral objectives. The information and skills taught in a course lead to a desired result or outcome. For example, if you want to teach learners how to create a document on a computer (desired outcome), you will need to teach them how to navigate the screen, insert and edit text, and format text (information and skills). If you want to teach learners how to be effective presenters, you will need to teach them how to prepare a presentation, develop a pleasant speaking voice, and hold the interest of the audience. Each example includes one overall outcome, and any number of skills that are required to accomplish that outcome.

Behavioral objectives, or *performance objectives*, name skills that learners need to be able to demonstrate by the end of the class. They provide the conditions under which the performance will be accomplished, and the level of accuracy required for successful completion of the performance. The information you gather from the needs assessment is the basis for identifying the objectives.

Although objectives bring direction and clarity to a situation, most people believe that objectives are difficult to write. That's because people tend to use words that they understand, not words that someone else might understand. And they often rely on facial expressions, gestures, and other forms of non-verbal communication to verify understanding. When you deliver information, you want people to understand what you are talking about. But how do you know they understand? What did they do to verify understanding? Did they nod their heads, smile in a certain way, or give some other clue? If so, are you sure they interpreted your message correctly? And did you interpret their clues correctly? The key is *performance*—what do you want learners to clearly demonstrate? Understanding cannot be performed; skills can be performed. Remember, if you cannot physically do it, then it is not a performance.

Your objectives should be clear and easy to understand. And they should reflect a high level of thinking. The table below shows the hierarchy of cognitive skills. You'll notice that the lowest level is *knowledge*. Knowledge is demonstrated through memorization. For example, a test for knowledge might ask learners to list the steps to open a document in a specified word processing program. Learners are required to recite steps. This is knowledge, the lowest level in the table. *Comprehension* requires the learner to be able to discuss the concept, but it is still not proof of learning. *Application* requires the learner to apply the new concept to other situations. Learners need to reach this level if they are to use your training information back at their workplaces. *Analysis* requires the learner to compare and contrast the ideas in this concept with other ideas. The next level is *synthesis*. You want the learner to be able to use the new information to design or build other ideas. And finally, you want the learner to *evaluate* the new information. Learners can invent new ways and new concepts. Your goal is to move learners to more cognitive skills in the table. Refer to this table often when you write your objectives. What level are your objectives? Are learners expected to list the steps in a procedure, or will they apply the new concept to other situations? Always strive for the high end of the table.

Table of Cognitive Skills

Skill Levels	Performance Examples
1 Knowledge	Write, define, name, list
2 Comprehension	Restate, discuss, describe, explain, translate, locate
3 Application	Operate, illustrate, use, draw
4 Analysis	Compare, contrast, calculate, solve
5 Synthesis	Compose, design, construct
6 Evaluation	Rate, estimate, measure

Writing objectives doesn't have to be difficult. People will get the most out of your training event if you use a needs assessment and the table of cognitive skills, and prepare instructionally and physically for class. This preparation forms the foundation of your training event. Now you can develop the materials and set the schedule for the class.

Often course objectives are confused with course descriptions. Course descriptions describe a process or procedure, while course objectives describe a performance. Although course descriptions often provide valuable information and tell you what the course is about, they do not tell you what the learner will accomplish by the end of the course.

As mentioned in the definition, performance objectives have three components: performance, conditions, and criterion. Now let's look at examples of a description and an objective and contrast them. Objectives tell you what a successful learner will be able to do by the end of the course. They also tell you the conditions and levels of accuracy required for success. Do you think this statement is a description or an objective? *Using a computer and a word processing program, learners will type text from a sample letter provided. Learners are not expected to type accurately. They will correct their typing errors as part of the activity.* This is an objective. There are required performances (typing text; correcting errors), there are stated conditions under which the learner will perform (using a computer and a word processing program), and there is an explanation of how well the learner must perform (not expected to type accurately). Now try this statement. *Learners create a document, insert and delete text, and format their documents.* This is a course description. It describes the information included in the course. It does not provide the conditions under which learners will perform, or the level of accuracy that is required.

Writing Objectives

Remember—there are three requirements for every objective: performance, conditions, and criterion. To make sure that all of your objectives are clear and useful, you should follow the same steps each time. This will help you meet all three requirements for an objective, and you will be able to quickly locate any problems.

1. **Performance**: What do you want the learner to be able to do?

2. **Conditions**: Under what conditions will the learner perform?

3. **Criterion**: How well must the learner perform?

Here is a model for objectives:

> *Given a set of specific **conditions** that enable the learner to perform, the learner will **perform** the action that demonstrates the desired result, with a specified accuracy or **criterion**.*

Using the model, consider these examples. When you write your objectives, check to see if you have information for each component in the model. If not, identify the missing component and then complete your objective.

> ***Example #1**: Using the white board, markers, and ruler in the front of the room, you will be able to draw a red circle that measures 12" in diameter.*

- **Performance**: draw a circle

- **Condition**: the white board, markers, and ruler are in the front of the room

- **Criteria**: the circle is red and measures 12" in diameter

> *Example #2*: *Given two boards, a hammer, and six nails, apprentices will nail the boards together in three minutes. All of the nails must be hammered into the boards.*

- **Performance:** nail the boards together

- **Condition:** two boards, a hammer, and six nails

- **Criteria:** complete the job in three minutes, with all of the nails hammered into the boards

The words "be able to" do not affect the validity of your objectives. Whether or not you use the phrase in your objectives is based on your personal preference. Some people like to use "be able to" because the words indicate that the learner has successfully performed the skill and can perform the skill again upon demand. Others prefer to omit the phrase. They contend that it does not verify that successful performance has taken place. Instead, it suggests ability. There is no proof that the performance has taken place.

Properly written objectives contain more information than one sentence can handle. And crowding the components into one sentence sometimes makes the sentence difficult to read and understand. Don't be afraid to use two or three sentences to express your intent for learning. It's better to have a lengthy objective that has all three components than a short objective that is missing information.

An objective must be *measurable*. In other words, you must be able to verify that the learner can and has completed the performance. You'll notice that the words in the left column of the following table are clear and meaningful. They are performances. The words in the right column are fuzzy and vague. They require a performance. When you write objectives, use clear, meaningful words to describe the performance.

Performances	Fuzzy, vague words
write	understand
say	appreciate
create	recognize
add	comprehend
identify	know
construct	develop
solve	study
calculate	learn
list	value
draw	internalize
apply	consider

Objectives During the Design Phase

Objectives affect each stage of the training event. That is why they are so critical. Objectives tell you where you are going. Just as you use a road map to plan a trip, you use objectives to help you design your training event.

Suppose you are a trainer for a computer training center. You have been asked to conduct a training event for a local group. The assignment is to teach learners how to use a word processing application. You need to know which application they need to learn, and which features are important to them. This information helps you identify the content of the course, so you can select usable materials. By narrowing the scope of information, you can identify objectives that will enable you to accomplish your assigned goals. This information goes hand in hand with the needs assessment to properly identify needs, expectations, and objectives.

Objectives During Implementation

After the training event begins, you need to continue to follow the objectives and monitor the progress of your plan. The objectives are your road map. Not only do they provide instructional direction, but they also provide learners with direction. When you get into your car and start the engine, don't you want to know where you're going? Do you go straight ahead or do you need to turn the car around? If you don't know where you are going, you might need to make several stops and ask for directions, when you could have been enjoying the scenery. Likewise, if learners don't know where they are going, they might spend too much time trying to find out where they are, when they could be learning. Amidst the confusion, learners might be missing important information. Both you and the learners need assurance that everything is going according to plan.

Objectives During Evaluation

How useful was your road map? Did you follow expressways, wishing you had taken the scenic route? Were the roads in good condition? Did you arrive at your destination on time and ready to enjoy your vacation?

Every trainer wants his or her training event to be successful. And a big part of that success comes from planning. Objectives are a key part of the planning, implementing, and evaluating processes. You need to know where you are going and how you will get there. What is the end result you expect to accomplish in the training event? And what is required to accomplish that end result? Then you need to know if your plan is working properly so far. And finally, you need to know if your plan was a good one, or if you need to adjust it for next time. At the end of your training event, go over your objectives again with the learners. Have you met all of your objectives? Is everyone satisfied with the results of the objectives? Just as you discuss the objectives with learners before class, discuss the objectives again at the end of class to confirm the end results. But you should not wait until the end of the training event to check your progress. Checking progress should occur throughout the class session. Practice activities and testing are two ways to check progress during the training event. Offer practice activities during the session. And test often to help learners gauge their progress, and to help you monitor your own style and pacing.

Preparing for Class

Always be prepared. If you fail to plan, you plan to fail.

Preparation is the key to a successful training event; it's like warm-up exercises that you complete before you begin a sporting event. (As we discussed in Chapter 1, "The Complexity of Adult Learning," examples and metaphors help adults relate new information to familiar information. And you are experiencing that technique now.) Exercises limber up your body, familiarize you with the surroundings, and help you focus on the game. Class preparation consists of exercises you do to relieve tension, get used to the surroundings, and focus on the training event. First you examine the materials you will be presenting; then you arrange the classroom and set up your hardware and props; and last but certainly not least, you deal with your anxiety. After you complete your warm-up exercises, you are ready to begin the class.

Preparing Instructionally for Class

In most training situations, you need to learn as much about the subject matter as possible in a short amount of time. Set realistic expectations for your preparation. You most likely will not have time to learn everything there is to know about the subject matter. On the other hand, not preparing is like trying to get to a specific location in a large city without directions or a road map.

To prepare instructionally for class, follow this five-step process. Although this process is designed for computer training events, you can modify it for other types of training.

1. Using the manual that learners will use in class, key through the course. Jot down anything that you find confusing or difficult to understand. This can include any area, such as concepts, vocabulary words, and procedures. You are already helping learners by identifying areas where they might experience difficulty during the training event.

2. When you finish, take your list to another trainer who has taught this course before, or to a subject matter expert. After discussing the items on your list, ask the trainer or subject matter expert, "What are 10 questions that people frequently ask in this course?" This gives you a head start on the information you should know to answer questions that people might ask during the training event.

3. Research the software and documentation. Experiment with tasks that interest you but are not included in the course. This helps you prepare for creative thinkers, who generally want to experiment with new procedures in different situations. And you will be able to point out some tricky areas in the software. Essentially, you are designing a practice activity that requires learners to use their new skills. Keep in mind that adult learners have experiences that make them valuable resources. You can always learn something new from them.

4. If this course is part of a series, such as an introductory-level course, key through the next course in the series, such as an advanced-level course. This helps you prepare for conceptual thinkers, who might ask advanced questions

about features not covered in the course. And you will be able to tell learners what they can look forward to in the next level of this course.

5.   Practice, practice, practice. Good trainers know the importance of practice. Learners will quickly notice if you are not prepared, and you will lose credibility. Remember, adult learners are seeking new information. If the information does not hold truth and relevancy, they will immediately dismiss it. They value every minute, so you need to make the most of your training time. Rarely do you get a second chance.

Practice involves more than one rehearsal. Begin by teaching the course to yourself and work your way through the following four stages of practice. By the time you complete step 4, the dry run, you will know the material and be confident presenting the information.

1.   **Mirroring:** At this stage of practice, you are teaching the course to yourself. You are only concerned with saying the words this time. So you can use an empty room, stand in front of a mirror, or you can even do this in your car when you travel. Don't just think the words, say them—make them come out of your mouth. Just thinking the words to yourself, not speaking out loud, robs you of important feedback—your own. And it changes the focus of the feedback in your other practice sessions. Observers will be focusing on issues that you should have already noticed and improved upon based on your own feedback.

2.   **Verbal run:** This step involves at least one other person, such as a friend, spouse, or another trainer. When you teach the course this time, you are looking for feedback about what you are saying, not how you are saying it. Focus on the technical aspects of the material, but don't expect to know everything there is to know about the subject. Are your listeners confused? Are you demonstrating a clear understanding of the subject matter?

At the end of this event, you should feel comfortable with the subject matter, knowing that you are technically prepared.

3. **Desert run:** Now teach the course to yourself again, but this time use the classroom where the training will take place. This way you can get used to the room, set a comfortable environment, and check the equipment and noise level. If for some reason you cannot use the classroom designated for the training, use another classroom to simulate the event. If your teaching involves travel, get there early so you have time for this step. You don't want to arrive late at the training site, only to find that the room is far too small for the event. And what if your style is to move around the room while you teach? You need time to practice teaching in the environment without tripping over cords or people's belongings. Chances are, if you aren't comfortable in the space, learners won't be comfortable either.

4. **Dry run:** This time you are teaching the course to several people, who are playing the role of the learners. Try to have at least one other trainer at this event. Focus on your presentation. When you teach the course this time, you are looking for feedback about your presentation and delivery of the information. Are you helping learners relate the information to familiar situations? Are you using techniques that are comfortable for the people in your class? Are you varying your techniques to allow for other learning styles? At the end of this event, you should be ready to teach the course. You know the material and you are confident about your presentation.

Preparing the Classroom

Arrange to see the classroom before the day of the training event. Many factors affect your presentation, such as lighting, room size, seating arrangement, equipment, and temperature control. You might find that you need to request equipment for the event, or you might need to bring your own equipment. And you will need time to practice teaching in the room to adjust to the environment. Consider your teaching style and the type of training you are presenting when you examine the room. If you feel comfortable and relaxed, learners will be able to relax and enjoy the training event. But if you are not comfortable, or if you are preoccupied with problems concerning the classroom setup, you and the people in your class will not be focused on the subject matter.

If you properly prepare for class, the sky is the limit—you can succeed even if you have a small, stuffy classroom and the power goes off. You can do this by separating the things you can control from the things you cannot control. Adjust the things you can control, but accept and deal with the things you cannot control. This way you can focus on the training event in a positive light instead of focusing on the negative, which puts a dark cloud over the event. Furthermore, adult learners want you to succeed. By attending this training, they are demonstrating their need for the information that you have prepared.

The setup of the classroom can affect the learning environment. Notice how interaction differs when you use different room arrangements. You can facilitate or hinder learning depending on the amount of interaction you encourage among participants. The arrangement of the classroom also affects your availability to learners, and it can influence the effectiveness of visual aids. Consider whether you want to be the focus, or you want learners to work together to solve problems and discuss issues. Assuming you have choices in the classroom setup, consider the following room arrangements.

- *Theater or Assembly style:* minimal interaction between the group and the presenter, no hands-on activities, commonly used for lecture format.

Theater (Assembly) style

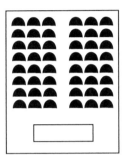

The room is arranged with chairs in straight rows, similar to those in a movie theater or assembly hall. There are no desks or tables. This style is common for lectures and suggests one-way communication. It discourages interaction and hands-on activities. The focus is on you, the presenter. The pressure is greater for you to keep your presentation exciting and motivating. Otherwise, learners quickly and easily become bored and restless.

- *Classroom style:* interaction between the presenter and the group, hands-on activities, commonly used for instructor-led format.

Open Classroom style

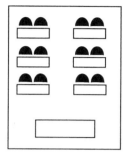

In the *Open Classroom style,* desks are arranged side by side with space between them. Each pair of learners is like an island. They might interact with the presenter, but rarely with other pairs of learners. The focus is on the presenter.

Closed Classroom style

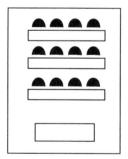

In the *Closed Classroom style,* desks are arranged in rows. Each row of learners is a group that works together. The groups might interact with the presenter, and with other participants in their groups. But there is little interaction among groups. The focus of each group is on the presenter.

Chevron style

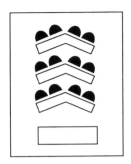

The *Chevron style* is similar to the Closed Classroom style. However, each row of desks is turned slightly to form a chevron. This shape encourages more group interaction and peer facilitation. The focus of each group is on the presenter.

- *Conference style:* This style includes several variations.

  Conference table style: interaction among the participants in the group, hands-on activities, commonly used for group-directed format.

Conference table style

This style encourages communication among the people in the group. The presenter assumes the role of facilitator. Because the learners can see each other, group interaction is strong. The focus is spread between the presenter and the group. When considering this style, keep in mind that seating at the table is not evenly distributed. Either end of the table can be seen as the "head of the table," which suggests a leadership role that might be intimidating.

U-shape style: interaction among the participants in the group and the presenter, hands-on activities, commonly used for group-directed format.

U-shape style

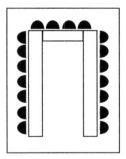

This style encourages more communication among the people in the group. Most of the learners can see each other without turning around. The presenter can move freely in and out of the group. The focus is spread between the presenter and the group. If you like to move around when you teach, and you like to be part of the group, you might consider using this style.

Closed square style: interaction among the participants in the group, hands-on activities, commonly used for group-directed format.

Closed square style

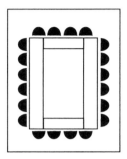

This style encourages open communication among the participants in the group. The presenter assumes the role of facilitator and functions outside the group. The focus is on the participants in the group, not on the facilitator. This style is useful when you have topics that you want to assign to the group, or when you want them to brainstorm ideas and hold group discussions to resolve problems or issues.

Hexagon style: interaction among participants in the group, hands-on activities, commonly used for group-directed format.

Hexagon style

This style is similar to the closed square. It encourages open communication among the participants in the group and assumes that the presenter is a facilitator, functioning outside the group. The focus is on the participants as they brainstorm ideas and hold group discussions to resolve problems and issues.

Herringbone style: interaction between the presenter and each group of learners, hands-on activities, commonly used for group-directed format.

Herringbone style

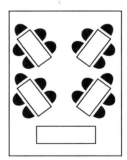

This style focuses on small group interaction. The presenter is seen as the facilitator, and each table group works as a unit. Communication among the participants at different tables is minimal. This style is useful for competition among groups.

V-shape style: interaction between the presenter and the group, hands-on activities, commonly used for instructor-led format.

V-shape style

This style focuses on the presenter. The tables, which enable hands-on activities, are arranged in one large chevron shape. Although this arrangement encourages interaction among the participants in the group, it is not a high level of interaction because all participants face the presenter.

- *Banquet style:* interaction among participants in the group, hands-on activities, commonly used for group-directed format.

Banquet style

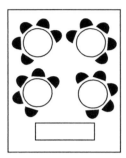

This style is used mostly for group discussions. Because the participants are typically seated at a round table, participants can see each other. The focus is on the group, with a high degree of interaction. The presenter can either be part of the group or act as the facilitator. The use of audio and visual aids is not recommended in this style because there isn't any place in the room where placement of the equipment does not cause sight and sound problems for some participants.

Before you accept the arrangement of the classroom or rearrange it, think about the activities you have planned. Will your plans work in this setting? Consider your teaching style. Do you often like to move around in the room? Consider the goals for the training event. Do you expect to engage learners in discussions and activities, and encourage them to play an active role in their learning? These are questions you should answer as part of your assessment of the facilities.

Rely on checklists to make sure you have all the necessary materials for the training event. Include *all* items, such as your manual, on your Materials Checklist, even though you're sure you'll "never forget them." Also include "just in case" items that you might not be able to get at the last minute, such as a light bulb for the overhead projector. After you create your checklist, make several copies and have one handy for each training event.

✓ Materials Checklist

___ Business cards

___ Eraser

___ Evaluation forms

___ Extension cords

___ Instructor's manual

___ Student manual

___ Name cards (tent cards)

___ Overhead projector

___ Overhead projector bulb

___ Blank video tape

___ VCR

___ Video camera

___ Travel folder

___ Welcome letter

Equally important is the Tear-Down Checklist. This guarantees a successful setup for the next class. Hardware problems are expected occasionally, but you should make it part of your procedure to leave the facility in the order you found it. After all, you expect the same courtesy when you arrive at the facility.

✓ Tear-Down Checklist

____ Return diskettes to boxes

____ Return templates to boxes

____ Check all drives and remove diskettes

____ Turn off all equipment

____ Remove used paper from printer and realign

____ Straighten chairs and pick up litter

____ Return unused manuals to inventory

____ Clean whiteboards

____ Clean instructor station area

____ Hand in evalutations

Preparing Physically for Class

Your health and physical well-being are important. You heard the words as a child, and you'll continue to hear them as an adult: *Eat healthy foods and get plenty of rest*. Training is exhausting work and it is important for you to be mentally and physically prepared. As a child, you probably found it difficult to concentrate on your school work when you were tired, or when you hadn't eaten breakfast. It's just as difficult as an adult. And now, people are counting on you to enlighten them with new information. Even though training is exhausting, it is motivating and rewarding, because you are sharing information that excites you. But it is difficult to be focused and enthusiastic when you are tired or feeling ill.

Wear comfortable, professional clothing. Before the training event, find out what attire learners are expected to wear. If you are not comfortable with the clothes you are wearing, you will be directing the focus of the event to your clothing instead of the subject matter.

Presentation Skills

Sad but true, public speaking rates higher than death on a list of fears. (How can that be when you have total control over your speaking skills?) And what might go wrong during your presentation? You might be late due to a traffic jam or a delayed flight. Your luggage might not arrive on time. You might lose your note cards or misplace your manual. Or you might arrive and find that the equipment promised is not in the classroom. Any of these problems can easily cause you to panic.

Preparation is the key to conquering your fears. If you followed the steps in this chapter to prepare your training event—learned the subject matter, practiced your presentation, and maintained your checklists— you have taken care of the things you can control. The rest, as they say, is a cake walk. Well, certainly not that easy, but your preparation has given you the confidence to succeed. You know your "stuff." Now you can polish your style and work on new ways to motivate and excite learners.

Here are a few tips to help you polish your style:

- Practice speaking in a firm, clear voice. Use varying volume and pitch as you emphasize important points. You want to be easily heard, but not to sound loud or unpleasant. Your voice should be conversational.

- Express a warm, confident, enthusiastic feeling through your voice and your mannerisms. Avoid a dry or lecturing tone, and avoid self-inflation (ego tripping).

- Use appropriate vocabulary. Keep in mind that many adults are unfamiliar with terms that are common to you, such as download or module. Use clear, everyday language, and define technical terms as you use them.

- Use humor cautiously. Humor can be refreshing when you use it appropriately, and adults prefer to learn in a relaxed, informal environment. So you might want to use humor to break the ice or lighten your presentation. But don't overdo it. Limit the amount of humor you use, and avoid offensive or distasteful material. It's best to go with the saying, "If in doubt, leave it out." Otherwise, you risk losing credibility as a professional. And if humor isn't your style, don't force it. Instead, look for humorous situations that occur naturally. Often you can find a relevant cartoon or joke and project it on the screen. Typically, you have one person in your class who is naturally humorous. Direct a cue to that person, and watch what happens. You will see a high level of participation. Humorous people are often hams and like to have the floor now and then. So they will pay close attention to you because they don't want to miss a cue.

- Be aware of your body language and how it affects other people. Adults prefer a trainer who is active; that is, standing instead of sitting, and moving around moderately instead of staying in one place. However, excessive pacing and wild hand waving is not well received. You might prefer to move around the classroom while you teach, but others might find that distracting. One approach is to make a mental drawing of a "staging area," a circle about five feet in diameter. Your workstation, projection device, flip chart, and so on, should be within or at the perimeter of this area. Also, try to confine your movements to the staging area. And smile; it looks good on you.

- If you prefer to teach from the back of the room, deliberately move to the front now and then for a brief demonstration or discussion. Some people are not comfortable with the trainer in the back of the room. You might also want to approach individual workstations occasionally to check on students' progress and help them with problems.

- Link with the people in your class. *Linking* is simply connecting with learners. Be aware of their problems and needs by watching for signs of approval or disapproval, acceptance or rejection, and agreement or disagreement. When you know that the learners are receiving the material positively, you can safely enhance your presentation with additional information or items of particular interest. You can establish linking in the following ways:

  - Watch for signs of frustration, resistance, or confusion. Facial expressions, body language, and lack of participation in hands-on activities are clues to a person's feelings.

  - Listen for excessive computer beeping, errant keystrokes, loud sighs, and negative remarks as expressions of discontent.

  - Check in with learners to establish the appropriateness of your pace and the clarity of your presentation. Summarize and review topics to measure clarity. If necessary, re-teach information and adjust your pace.

  - Encourage class participation. Solicit questions and comments and address individual problems whenever possible. People will eagerly participate if you handle questions positively and enthusiastically.

We've all seen trainers who are seasoned professionals. They perform perfectly every time—they are inspiring. And they look like they're having fun. Yet when you ask them how they make it look so easy, they'll tell you they were scared silly. After such a smooth performance, how can that be? The key to successful training is preparation—a prepared trainer is a confident trainer.

Seven Steps to Becoming a Star Trainer

Successful trainers design training events that meet the needs of the learners. Knowing your audience is fundamental to your design.

1. Relate new information to familiar information. Adults are responsible for their own learning. Although you cannot make them learn, you can help them make good decisions about their learning. As part of your planning, assess the needs of the people you will be training. (See Chapter 3, "Needs Assessment.") Make sure the training objectives match the needs of the learners. Then, when you present the new information during the training event, point out areas that learners will find familiar. Help them find relevance and relationship in the new information. This way, they can accept responsibility for their learning.

2. Provide practice activities. Adults learn by doing. People remember 5 to 10 percent of what they see, 30 to 50 percent of what they see and hear, 50 to 70 percent of what they say, and 70 to 90 percent of what they say and do. For every new skill, provide an activity so learners can practice. Use real-world activities that create a challenge. That way, learners can apply their new skills to problems they have at work. Adults often like to share their problems and solutions.

3. Provide critical information before "nice to know" information. Adults learn what they need to know. Because adults are problem-centered and results-oriented, they take

in everything they believe they need to know. In most cases, they will avoid the "nice to know" information for now because it does not hold immediate relevancy for them. Yet, in a few months, they might be very interested in the same information they dismissed today. Typically adults like "just in time" information—it's there when they need it. When you design a training event, include critical information in the body of the training event. Then, offer "nice to know" information as an option during non-critical times, such as breaks or after the event.

4. Use real-world problem-solving activities. Adults like problem-centered learning. When you provide practice activities, use case studies and real business problems, and let adults solve them. They like to use their new skills to solve other problems. And they want to do it themselves. For some people, it's like a crossword puzzle. They can't put it down until they finish it.

5. Encourage learners to share their experiences. Adults learn from experience. The most valuable examples of applying new skills are those from people's real experience. Adults can provide scenarios and horror stories based on their experience. Let the learners solve problems together by sharing their experiences and using their new skills.

6. Create a relaxed, informal atmosphere. Adults prefer to learn in an informal atmosphere, so you should try to create one. Sometimes formality breeds hostility. Informality helps everyone in the group feel like they're working from the same level. This way, learners are relaxed and ready to learn.

7. Vary your style and teaching tools. Adults prefer variety in their learning. Group participation and lecture are two opposite styles, but they are both effective tools when used in the proper setting. You can also put some spice in your training by using artwork or visual aids. If you don't feel

adept at artwork, you might visit informally with learners before class to see if there are artists in the class who enjoy showing off their talents. If so, you can add not only artwork and spice to your training event, but also participation that demonstrates understanding. A word of caution about asking learners to participate in artistry, demonstrations, or other types of displays involving other learners: always ask a person's permission privately ahead of time. Don't put them on the spot in class. And don't assume that just because Joe has a great sense of humor, he will want to get up in front of the class. You could destroy trust and alienate the people in your class.

Anxiety

Every trainer experiences a certain amount of fear and uneasiness before class—even veteran trainers. But how do professionals manage to look so calm and relaxed, as if they are enjoying every moment? In a nutshell, they *are* enjoying every moment, because they have mastered the art of channeling their anxiety.

Like clockwork, anxiety rears its ugly head moments before every class. Sometimes it's a consuming feeling of fear; other times it's nausea or sweaty palms. And no matter what you do, you cannot escape it. Does this sound familiar? You're not alone. You need a plan—a routine exercise to follow before each class. Some people like to take a few short breaths before they begin; others like to take a deep breath. Still others like to engage in informal conversation to take their mind off the presentation, while some like to concentrate on the subject matter.

You will find what works best for you as soon as you accept your anxiety in a positive light. Those butterflies before your presentation are a clue that your preparation is under way. As Les Donaldson and Edward E. Scannell so eloquently put it, the trick is to make the "butterflies fly in formation". If you make time to deal with your anxiety, you can turn it into positive energy to motivate yourself and your class. Encourage anxiety; it's healthy.

The real cause for concern is the *lack* of anxiety. Without it, you cannot maintain your energy level. Ask yourself, "Am I enthusiastic about what I'm doing?" If not, you might be experiencing burnout. Monitor your energy level to be sure. Then take steps to rekindle your spirits and enthusiasm. Perhaps it's time for a new direction in your career. Adults typically change careers as many as seven times, and that number seems to be growing. More importantly, you need to pay attention to your needs, and follow your instincts. You'll find more discussion about burnout in Chapter 9, "The Burnout Blues."

By simply changing your philosophy about anxiety, you are moving in the right direction. Instead of using the word "anxiety," use another term such as "mental aerobics." You can choose any name for your mental preparation; it's all yours. It's your special way of being a star trainer every time. The next time you have a training event, follow the steps to learn the material, practice your presentation, and check the classroom setup. Then do your *aerobics*. For example, suppose you decide that your *aerobics* are to meditate and then take a few short breaths before each training event. You arrive at the training site the day before the event. After checking the hardware setup, you practice your presentation to get comfortable in the environment. On the day of the training event, you arrive early and check to make sure the setup is the same. Then allow yourself 30 to 45 minutes (or whatever time you feel comfortable with) for your *aerobics*. Find a room where you can be alone, and do your *aerobics*. Just before you leave the room, say out loud, "I am prepared. I am a star." Now smile. You'll be surprised at how much this can lift your spirits and motivate you for the event.

It's nice to be in the room a little while ahead of the participants. That way, you can welcome them when they arrive. Remember how frightening it was as a child to enter a new classroom on the first day of school each year? Well, for participants, this is similar. People feel comfortable and relaxed if you're there to greet them with a pleasant smile. They get an immediate sense of belonging.

Chapter Six

Conceptual Learning;
Delivery Techniques

*Tell them how and they wonder why; explain why
and they know how.*

Which should you teach—concepts or procedures? The answer is
concepts. As we discussed in Chapter 1, "The Complexity of Adult
Learning," adults decide whether or not to accept new information based
on the three Rs: relevancy, relationship, and responsibility. Adults like to
be responsible for their own learning. If the new information is not
timely and appropriate, and if it does not relate to the learner's needs,
then it will be rejected. Procedures are logical steps based on concepts.
Until you learn the concept, the procedures hold little meaning.

Suppose you work on the assembly line at ABC Technologies. Your
company makes and assembles parts for different types of engines.
When the product gets to your work area on the assembly line, you
attach a rubber ring to an opening and then place the product back on
the assembly line. You don't know how you contribute to the product
other than attaching a rubber ring. You don't even know what part of the
engine you are working on. No one told you that this rubber ring is part
of a car engine and is being questioned by safety experts. If you had
known this information, you could have offered suggestions based on
your experience. This is part of the same fixture that you modified on
your own car engine. If you had seen the finished product, and received

information about the design of the product and the stages of construction, you might have been able to contribute to the process and design stages. Understanding the concept—the what and the why—helps you effect a better process and product.

In today's business world, there is a demand for workers to accomplish more with less. Feeling the crunch, people rush through training and expect to hit the ground running when they return to work. Learners think they don't have time for concepts; they just want survival skills. They tend to put the cart before the horse. But remember, you're the expert. People need the big picture before they learn the procedure, and the concept is the big picture. In reality, learners don't simply follow the steps in a procedure time after time to complete their work. There is more involved in the learning process. Learners modify the steps so that they can use them in different situations. This requires a high level of understanding. Memorizing steps is the lowest level, which is knowledge. (See Chapter 4, "Objectives that Work.")

Another advantage of teaching the concepts first is that learners retain the information longer. If you start with concepts, the procedures make sense to learners, and they can apply the new information to a variety of situations. Even if they don't use the new information again for a long period of time, learners will be able to pick up where they left off because the concept makes sense to them. They can figure out the steps based on their understanding and application of the concepts.

The Concept Tree

How do you deliver concepts to learners who think they want only survival skills? Learners, by nature, are results oriented, so they often become anxious for procedures. They know where they are going, and they simply want to get there as quickly as possible. They don't realize the importance of concepts. But you've assessed the situation and you know how to deliver the information that adults need and want. By starting with the big picture, you give learners an overview that they can use to begin the process of relating this new information to similar information from previous experiences. As your overview begins to stir a sense of understanding in learners, they say to themselves, "Oh, I get it. It's like the information I learned a few months ago." At this level of understanding, learners have reached a critical comfort level. Now they are ready to experience higher levels of learning.

When we present concepts in our classrooms, we follow a model that we call the "concept tree." Concepts are a hierarchy of thoughts and ideas, each one building on another. The concept tree is similar to a family tree. You can draw the tree growing up or down. The tree starts at the trunk with the eldest family member. Generations are represented as branches. For example, if you want to teach word processing, you start with "word processing" at the trunk of the tree. The main topics that you include in the word processing course are the main branches of the tree (navigating, editing, formatting, page layout, proofing tools, and printing). Each topic contains several skill areas that are smaller branches attached to the main branches; for example, proofing tools include the spell checker, thesaurus, and grammar checker. Generations of topics continue from branch to branch (parent to child) and finally to the leaves, which is where you will find the basic steps that are the result of each concept. The steps, or leaves, are at the end of the concept tree (see the Print Preview branch). Just as the tree must develop branches before it has leaves, learners must learn concepts before they can understand procedures. You wouldn't teach people how to undo a command before you teach them to use the command. And you wouldn't teach someone how to change the print area before they learn how to create and print a document. By first learning the concept of printing, learners can identify a need for print area settings.

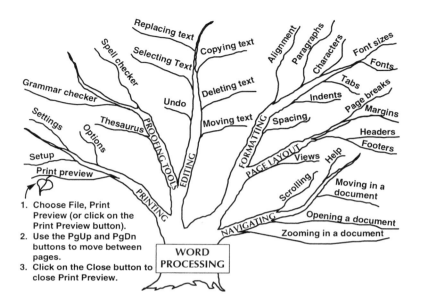

The concept tree is not always perfectly proportioned. Its layout depends on the components of the concept. For example, our PC Literacy course offers an irregular illustration. At the trunk of the tree is the question, "What is a computer?" There are two types of computers: mainframes and personal computers. Personal computers extend to software and hardware. Hardware is made up of input, output, processor, and storage. Software is made up of applications and operating systems. Applications include custom and off-the-shelf products, such as databases, word processing, spreadsheets, graphics, utilities, language, and groupware. As you can see from the following illustration, this concept tree is much more complex.

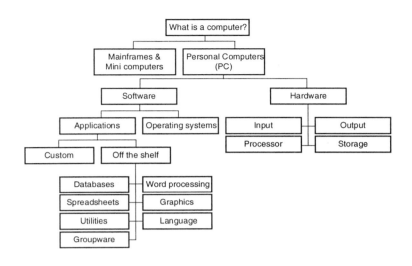

Setup/Delivery/Follow-up

Effective concept building enables learners to easily grasp new ideas, processes, and procedures. Concepts start at the foundation, or setup, which sets the stage for the delivery. The setup might be an analogy, or it might be a question that starts a discussion and leads to discovery. Although the trainer starts the setup, learners often take the lead and become heavily involved right away. Eager to test the new concept, learners often ask questions or make comments that contribute to a smooth transition to the delivery. The delivery, under the direction of the trainer, includes group participation. Learners test the new procedures based on the concept. The follow-up belongs to the learners. It is the culmination of information learned in the setup and delivery. Learners demonstrate their skills and understanding by performing procedures and, more importantly, by sharing other ways to use the new skill. They relate the new concept to familiar concepts. The setup/delivery/follow-up procedure is a cycle of concept building that continues through the training event.

Setup/Delivery/Follow-up

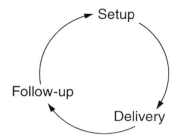

Setting up a Concept

A successful setup motivates learners and sets the stage for the delivery. It gives people a sense of direction, and it creates a bridge from new and unfamiliar information to information that is already familiar. But some concepts don't require a lot of setup. And there can be a danger in providing too much setup. How much is too much? Of course, the amount and type of setup depends on the learners' needs and skill levels. As you become more experienced, you will be able to identify how much setup to provide. Your assessment of learners' needs and expectations before and during class will help you determine the appropriate level of setup.

For example, if you want to teach novice computer users how to write macros, you don't begin by saying, "Write a macro that inserts your company's name and address every time you type a specific key combination." Instead, you might start by defining a macro and explaining why it is a useful tool. Then you could ask learners to explain some tasks that they would like to complete more efficiently. Interaction motivates people to learn about this new tool that will make them more efficient. And by sharing ideas, people will learn several ways to use macros. Often, learners don't realize the potential of the new tool. In this example, people are interacting and sharing ideas and experiences long before they learn how to perform the new skill.

There will be times when you need to use more than one technique. Because people are different, not all techniques work for everyone. If your training event includes people from different parts of the country, or people from other countries, you will need to pay close attention to different cultures, styles, and language barriers. If your class includes people from a variety of skill levels, you might need to use more than one technique to reinforce your teaching. See "Techniques for Setup, Delivery, and Follow-up" later in this chapter.

Delivering a Concept

Your delivery begins as soon as you create the link between the new concept and an idea that is familiar to learners. A successful delivery satisfies the learner's need for information. At this point, learners should know what the concept is, why it is important, and how they can use it effectively. Now they are ready to learn procedures and practice their new skills. And by working together, learners can share ideas and resolve existing and potential problems.

Although you can use several techniques to deliver a concept, we recommend hands-on practice because people learn best by doing. According to research, people learn 20% of what they hear, 30% of what they see, and 80% of what they do. But just practicing the new skills is not enough. Give learners an opportunity to find other ways to use their new skills. Use brainstorming activities to help learners think of other uses for the new information. Then have them test their ideas and transfer their new skills to other situations. Based on life and work experiences, adults often find several ways to use their new skills, whereas youths have little or no experience yet to relate to the new skills. In most cases, youths can only speculate about potential uses for the new information.

As you work through the delivery of new information, you will often find a need to slow down or speed up your pace (perhaps more than once during a training event). Advanced learners tend to move quickly through topics, while novices become easily overwhelmed. And a class with both advanced learners and novices will require more attention. You will need to find a way to provide challenge for advanced learners, and at the same time provide guidance and support for novice users.

To optimize the pace of your training day, consider these important points: the skill levels of the people in the class, critical versus optional material, and the amount of material you can cover by a particular time in the day compared to the amount of material you plan to cover during that time. In our classrooms, we use what we call the *AB technique*. The goal of the AB technique is to enable you to change the pace of your training and to teach both critical and optional tasks by the end of the day. It suggests that you review the content of the course ahead of time to decide which tasks are critical (A tasks) and which tasks are optional (B tasks). Tasks that contain shortcuts or reviews, and tasks that can be taught out of sequence, are typically labeled B tasks. Tasks that contain information, activities, and procedures that are critical to the concept being taught are labeled A tasks. Sometimes B tasks contain new and critical information that you defer because of the lack of time, need, or appropriate skill levels. Before the training day, mark each task in your manual accordingly.

As you begin your training day, tell people that "The manual contains additional material that might not be covered during the training day; however, all of the essential material in the manual will be covered." During the first quarter of your day, do all tasks (both A and B tasks). After the first break, if you realize that you are behind schedule, start covering only the A tasks. Re-evaluate your position at the next break and again at each succeeding break. Based on the learners' needs and skill levels, you might cover all tasks in one class, and cover only the A tasks in another class. At the end of the training day, if you have additional time, return to the B tasks. Based on the amount of time left in the day, you can teach the remaining material, demonstrate it, or ask learners to complete the material on their own after class for additional practice.

At times, you might be asked to participate in team teaching with a colleague. Team teaching is based on the premise that each trainer focuses on one area of delivery, thereby being better prepared and teaching from his or her strengths. Before you begin, explain to the class how team teaching works. Tell them what the role of each trainer will and will not be, and how you plan to use the front and the back of the room. Although team teaching suggests the potential for a gap between the teaching styles of the two trainers, this technique can be refreshing for learners. However, your style and the style of the other trainer should complement each other. Otherwise, you risk confusing the learners.

Styles that work well together are those that offer slight variations. A change in style should be pleasant and refreshing. For example, a trainer who is soft-spoken might be well-received during the early part of the training event, while a more energetic trainer provides a refreshing change for the latter part of the event when learners start to show signs of fatigue. Styles that do not work well together are those that are so different they clash. This makes the shift between training styles so drastic that learners concentrate on adapting to the style of the trainer rather than on the information the trainer is delivering. An energetic trainer who is constantly moving around the classroom, and whose voice projects loudly, keeping learners on the edge of their seats, should not be paired with a trainer who is extremely passive, and whose voice is so soft-spoken that people strain to hear. This pairing could result in difficulty for learners. A passive trainer should pair with a semi-energetic trainer. This way, the change from one trainer to the other is refreshing, yet not intrusive. The second trainer has more energy than the first, but not so much energy that he or she startles people. Most learners will enjoy at least one of the two styles used.

Following up a Concept

A successful follow-up shifts the focus from the trainer to the learners. Orchestrating the follow-up for each concept is the most critical part of the training event. As we pointed out in Chapter 2, "A Logical Approach to Training," you and the learners might be participating in the setup and delivery, but it is critical that the learners perform the follow-up. Remember, learners are responsible for their learning. If you perform the follow-up, you are testing yourself. And you will be responsible for their learning. Your goal is to give learners responsibility for their own learning.

How do you orchestrate a follow-up for learners to perform? There are several techniques you can use, such as questions, discussions, brainstorming, games, and other activities. You can choose from a variety of techniques and examples we have provided, or you can create your own follow-up activities. When you facilitate a follow-up activity, remember that your job is to guide learners. The learners perform the action of the activity.

Techniques for Setup, Delivery, and Follow-up

The techniques you use to set up, deliver, and follow up concepts are based on the information you gather from assessments before and during class. Depending on the concept you are delivering, some techniques work better than others. Because setup, delivery, and follow-up are continuous, you might occasionally use the same technique in all three areas. For example, to set up the concept of file management, you might use the analogy, "A disk is like a file cabinet." And when you deliver the concept, you might use the analogy, "A directory is like a drawer in the file cabinet, and a subdirectory is like a folder in the drawer." Your follow-up activity might be that learners make up some analogies for the concept they just learned. Try these techniques to set up, deliver, and follow up your concepts.

- **Analogy:** An analogy relates an abstract idea to a familiar object or situation. For example, a style is like a recipe. However, analogies don't explain concepts. They simply point out a relationship between the new concept and something familiar. Learners need to make a connection between the familiar and the unfamiliar before they can proceed with their learning. Otherwise, they will spend valuable time struggling with a way to make sense of the new information rather than learning the concept. For example, the computer's hard disk is a difficult concept for new users to grasp. You can use an analogy to help learners relate the hard disk to something that is familiar to them, such as a parking lot. Just as a parking lot has lines painted on it to identify places where you can park your car, a hard disk has areas reserved on it where you can store your documents. For more analogies, see the appendix, "Analogies for Computer Training."

- **Storyline:** A storyline or scenario provides a business-related example that learners can use to relate the new information to their work. For example, print merge is a useful word processing feature. It enables users to customize letters easily. But if you concentrate on the procedure to create a document and a list of names, and then perform the steps involved, learners might be confused. Consequently, they might not want to use print merge. Realizing that print merge is a valuable, yet confusing concept, we once developed a slide show to help learners understand the concept. The slide show illustrated each step in the procedure of print merge. It was a fine slide show, but learners were so confused by the time they finished that they said they would rather not customize their letters. In fact, they said they would rather create a separate letter for each recipient. But when we introduced the concept by asking how many people in the class had ever received a sweepstakes letter from Ed McMahon, people immediately made the connection to the concept they were starting to learn. Then they were anxious to know how to do print merge. We learned from our slide show project that we were making a mountain out of a mole hill. The learners could not use the procedures until they understood the concept. When learners become too

79

involved in the procedure, they lose sight of the end results.

- **Display results:** Display the results of the task you are teaching. Often, learners appreciate seeing the results before they perform the activity. It gives them direction and helps them move toward the objective. When you explain difficult concepts, such as print merge, you might want to use more than one tool to help learners make the transition to the new information. For example, provide a storyline to set the stage, and then display the results of the print merge. This way, learners can think about relevancy and relationship, and also see the results of the activity they will perform.

- **Problem solving:** Many adults like to solve problems. They like to apply their new skills to a variety of situations. Based on individual experiences, learners approach problems differently. Some of their most valuable learning comes from peers sharing experiences and ideas. For example, you might show learners how to create a spreadsheet. Then, have learners work in pairs to create a spreadsheet that they can use at their workplaces. When they finish, have them share their ideas. Instead of having only the spreadsheet they created, each learner will have several ideas for different spreadsheets based on different needs and situations.

- **Examples:** Appropriate examples clarify confusing information. Before you can teach novice computer users how to use databases, you need to explain what a database is and why it is useful. For example, a database is a collection of items that have something in common. Your telephone book is a database of names and addresses. Your refrigerator is a database of foods that require cold storage. Immediately, learners want to provide you with other examples. And this is your proof that they understand the concept you are explaining.

- **Explain why:** Explain why a concept is important. Sometimes a concept is so new to learners that you might not be able to relate it to something familiar. Although this is extremely rare, it does happen occasionally. If you don't explain why, learners will spend valuable time wondering why they would want to learn about this concept. The best way to explain a concept is by using a job-related situation. Explain why the concept is important in terms of how people can use it to be more efficient on the job. Help them realize why they need this new concept.

- **Transitions:** Provide a bridge between concepts to show how they relate to one another. For example, you might end your discussion about creating a document by saying, "Now that you've created a document, you might want to change the appearance of the document. Let's modify the document by changing the font size and type face." Learners can use their new skills to learn more skills.

- **Discovery:** Give learners an opportunity to explore unfamiliar areas. For example, the Copy command enables learners to insert specific information in more than one place without creating the information more than once. After the people in your class have learned this concept, you might ask them how you can remove the text from one area and place it in another. Discovery poses a situation based on a concept, and learners use that information to discover another concept. Problem solving is similar, except that each concept is presented first. Then learners use their understanding of the concept to solve related problems. Sometimes discovery yields new ideas that you might not be expecting. You can use discovery findings to help people in future classes.

- **Questioning:** The questions you ask should promote thinking, not recitation. Steps and rules are in the book, where learners can read them as needed. The key is to help learners identify which skills to use for each situation.

Questioning promotes involvement by the learners. They learn from each other's responses. If no one responds to your question, ask the question in another way. Perhaps your wording was confusing. To encourage interaction and involvement by all of the learners, remind people that they can answer questions freely, rather than raise their hands. Tell them it's okay for more than one person to answer a question, and that you welcome more than one answer to questions. If you want to direct a question to one individual, you should use that person's name at the end of your question. Placing the person's name at the end of your question is important because it lowers the stress of hearing your name called. To promote independent learning, give each person a chance to come up with his or her own solutions to questions. Everyone can learn from the variety of answers.

- **Interactive summary:** The key to interactive summary is the word "interactive." Ask learners to summarize what they have learned. Write their responses on the board or flip chart. Then have a group discussion to explain each concept. Learners will help each other with the explanations and interact to summarize the concepts.

- **Interactive overview:** This is similar to an interactive summary, except here learners explain the big picture and how the new concept relates to the rest of the course. This technique demonstrates understanding at a high level. Not only does it prove that the learner understands the concept, but it also demonstrates that the learner knows why the concept is important to the rest of the course, and that the learner has a sense of the direction of the course. People can learn from each other using this technique.

- **Test:** A test is written proof of learning. However, your test questions should not test memorization. Use high-level questions that require the learner to create something, such as a paper report, flow chart, or model that demonstrates an understanding of the new concept. To check the validity of your questions, refer to the table of skill levels in Chapter 4, "Objectives that Work." Practice activities and labs are excellent examples of the effective use of tests. Learners can enjoy the challenge of these activities without feeling the stress of tests.

Creativity

Children often ask "Why?" in an effort to satisfy their curiosity. How many times do you hear adults respond by saying "Because I said so"? The child finally gives up the quest to know why and rejects the new information that caused the curiosity. Adults experience this, too. If they can't first understand why, adults might reject the information.

To encourage creativity, incorporate activities into your training event, such as brainstorming, small group activities, games, role playing, skits, or values clarification exercises. Any situation that promotes a high level of thinking also promotes creativity. And you will find that the more creativity flows, the more you and the learners become energized.

Media tools

Media tools are aids that you can use to help people learn. Although there are many types of tools that you can use to supplement your presentation, you will find that some work better than others. And you will find that particular tools complement your style. The main thing to remember when you use media is that it is an aid; it cannot replace you. You, the trainer, are the presenter of information to the learners. Media is simply a tool to reinforce the information. And not all topics require the use of supplemental aids. If you use one or two effective slide shows during your training event, you can satisfy auditory and visual learners.

But don't overdo it. If you use several slide shows, such as one for every concept, you probably won't satisfy either group.

Auditory learners might succeed based on your presentation alone. However, visual learners need to see the information in a way that makes it crystal clear. "A picture is worth a thousand words."

Media has been a topic of much research in the 90's. If you keep an eye on the media trends, you'll find a variety of products that can enhance your presentation.

Classroom Management

An ounce of prevention is worth a pound of cure.

The way you manage the people in your training events directly affects your rate of success as a trainer. Classroom management is twofold: it uses prevention techniques to avoid potential problems, and control techniques to eliminate problems if they occur. In the first few minutes of class, you should set the tone by explaining your expectations, stating the direction of the course, and discussing your flexibility. It's like learning a new game. Everyone gathers and visits until the leader steps forward and explains the rules, giving hints and clues about the game. Then they begin playing the game. No one begins until the leader has explained the rules. So, until you explain your rules (expectations, direction, flexibility), people will continue to visit, act playfully, and probably distract others. The learners are simply demonstrating the uncertainty of your direction, or indicating that your direction is not meeting their needs. From time to time, you might need to review or adjust your direction based on the needs and expectations of the people in your class.

Preventing Behavior Problems

Just as children misbehave, so do adults. How can that be, you ask—especially if adults typically like to be responsible for their own learning?

While it's true that adults prefer to take charge of their learning, they rarely get the chance.

Since their early years in grade school, people have been trained to be dependent, passive learners. Based on their past experiences, learners assume that you are in charge and will not grant them independence. And most trainers lack the self-confidence required to risk giving learners control of their learning. What could go wrong? Lack of control, chaos, learners might not need you, or you could lose credibility. What could go right? Everything—independent learning, discovery learning, problem solving, motivation, and people working together and sharing ideas. For most trainers, the fear of what could go wrong outweighs what could go right. Instructor-led training is the most common type of training today. It focuses on the trainer as the leader and controller. Trainers have spent years studying adult learners to understand how they think and work, but so far it appears that trainers haven't followed through with their findings to encourage independent learning.

Everyone in your training event has different needs and expectations. And not everyone attends training on a voluntary basis. Some people want to learn skills needed for new jobs, while others attend training because their managers require them to attend. Training might be a last resort before job dismissal. Defensiveness, resistance to change, and disruption are all possible reactions. This is why you need information about the learners' needs and expectations before class. Chapter 3, "Needs Assessment," includes guidelines for assessing learners' needs and expectations before class. Chapter 5, "Preparing for Class," shows you how to use assessment information as you prepare for class.

Prevention techniques include assuming a leadership role, setting clear direction, remaining focused, and reinforcing appropriate behavior. As a leader, you are expected to set the climate and tone for the day by explaining appropriate behavior and expectations. You need to provide a clear direction to motivate learners to enthusiastically get started. Although digressing a little has a nice calming effect, try to be brief if you use this technique. Remain focused, keeping your objectives in mind. If the training event is scheduled to end at 4:00 p.m., people expect to finish at that time. Some topics are more interesting than others, making it difficult to get back on task. If this happens, suggest continuing the discussion after class for those who want to stay. Otherwise, you might not accomplish the objectives set for the event.

To command positive behavior, you need to model and reinforce positive behavior. Adults often get sidetracked with conversations during breaks. So it is not uncommon to see them return late after a break. At the start of every break, tell learners that you will be starting promptly at a specified time. And then be sure you do start at that time, even if only one person has returned. Otherwise, the message you meant to send, *time is important*, is interpreted as *time isn't important*. And it's nice to thank people for getting back on time and assure them that they will finish the training event on time. Another successful technique is to tell learners before break that if they want to come back from break five minutes early, you will be demonstrating some features beyond the scope of the course. Adult learners are generally excited about new features and tips. This method lets you provide additional information for those who are interested, and also meet your objectives.

Controlling Behavior Problems

Sometimes even the best prevention techniques cannot guarantee that you won't have behavior problems. A learner might be angry or frustrated about something that is out of your control. There could be problems at home, or something might have gone wrong on the way to the training event. If this happens, you might have to quietly and discreetly take the learner aside during a break and discuss the problem. Without prying, ask if there is anything wrong that you should be aware of. Ask if there is anything you can do to help. Most often, adults will cooperate with you. Maybe the learner didn't realize the effect of his or her actions. Maybe the learner should be dismissed from the event. Consider the following examples.

> **Example #1:** A person in a recent computer training event seemed distant and not interested in the course. She wasn't

participating in discussions or hands-on activities. Although she sat quietly, her lack of performance was disruptive to others in the class. What would you do in such a case? During break, the trainer discreetly approached her to find out if there was a problem. She had just received tragic news concerning her family, and she wasn't sure what to do. She had no idea that she was affecting everyone negatively.

Example #2: A person in a training class kept talking to others whenever the trainer attempted to speak. He was disrupting the class. What would you do? When approached by the trainer during break, the person explained that if he didn't improve his skills, he'd lose his job. And he was afraid to admit that he didn't understand the information in the course. His behavior was an act of panic. The trainer was able to bring in a facilitator to help the learner keep up with the rest of the class.

Example #3: A person in a training class seemed frustrated with the course. He wasn't participating in hands-on activities. What would you do? After considering the learner's questions and comments, the trainer determined that this learner was in the wrong class. He had not met the prerequisites for the course. Luckily, there was still time for him to switch to the class he needed.

In each example, the trainer resolved the problem positively by recognizing signals and attending to problems quickly and discreetly. These are real problems that trainers face in training events. Pay close attention to the learners. Whether they use appropriate or inappropriate signals, you need to recognize the cue that something is wrong. The longer you wait to attend to them, the more you risk not meeting your objectives or theirs. And that affects everyone in the class, not just one person. Approach behavior problems in a positive way, assuming the person does not mean to misbehave. This way, you have a better chance for resolution. Remember, negative attitudes breed more negative attitudes. You want to model the attitude you desire, a positive attitude.

On the negative side, there is an occasional person who does not fit the mold. He or she is not motivated, doesn't want to be in the training event, and refuses to cooperate. If you have exhausted your efforts to accommodate the person, and you are concerned about the situation negatively affecting others in the class, you need to take steps to remove the disturbance from the classroom. This is a delicate matter that deserves the attention of your supervisor. Your organization should have a plan in place for this type of situation. Find out what the proper procedure is before class. If there is no plan, ask your supervisor to implement one right away.

Here are some techniques you can use to help eliminate behavior problems. In most cases, discreetly speaking to the person about the inappropriate behavior works better than any other technique. It allows the person to correct the behavior, and it allows both you and the person to maintain credibility.

- Active ignoring. Sometimes you can reduce or eliminate inappropriate behavior by simply ignoring the person who is misbehaving. Proceed with training, and avoid eye contact with the problem person. Monitor the progress of this technique carefully. If ignoring the problem is not effective, it can lead to even more conspicuous behavior. If this happens, you'll need to try another technique to alleviate the problem. You might want to confront the person during the next break.

- Negative focus. You might be able to eliminate a behavior problem quickly by bringing attention to the disruptive person. If a small amount of negative attention does not eliminate the problem, don't pursue it using this technique. You risk damaging your credibility and that of the disruptive person.

- The silent drift. This technique is used often with young learners. Continue to teach as you move closer to the disruptive person, intentionally not bringing attention to the behavior. Because you are the primary center of attention, your physical presence next to the person transfers attention to that person. The attention is often enough to stop the undesirable behavior.

- The whole-group message. This technique involves announcing to the entire group that there is a problem, when the message is really meant for one or a few people. For example, "Some of you are having a conversation among yourselves, but your voices are too loud and distracting to the rest of the group." Generally, the person with the behavior problem will recognize the description of his or her behavior.

- Bogus concern. Sometimes you can make a comment to the person that infers concern, but really sends a message of control. For example, "Is everything all right in the back of the room?" This technique is also used often with young learners.

- Private confrontation. This technique should be used only as a last resort. It is a one-to-one direct request for the disruptive behavior to stop.

Each technique provides for a quick and discreet resolution. The disruptive person has an opportunity to correct his or her inappropriate behavior.

Special Problems

Unfortunately, problems don't occur at convenient times; they occur while you are teaching. Although it is distracting to you and the people in the class, you need to attend to the problem right away. If you encounter a problem, and you have exhausted all of your options, you might need to use direct and personal intervention. In those cases, consider the following steps before you take action:

1. Diagnose the problem. Remain calm while you consider the cause of the problem. Is this course meeting the disruptive learner's needs? Does the learner meet the prerequisites for the course? Always make your first assumption a positive one. Remember, negative attitudes breed more negative attitudes. And if there is a simple solution to the problem, you can attend to it quickly and move on with the training event.

2. Validate the problem. Try to understand the learner's situation. Did you assess the learner's needs? Is this course difficult for learners? Should you try a different style to present the information? Often people mask fear by being disruptive. In example #2 under "Controlling Behavior Problems," fear that misunderstanding the concepts being taught would lead to job dismissal caused the learner to panic and act inappropriately.

3. Provide alternatives. Find a way for the learner to be part of the learning process. For example, you might want to suggest that the learner follow along with the information without participating in the hands-on activities. Sometimes this is less threatening for someone who is struggling with new information.

4. Bring closure to the issue. Let the person know that unless a new problem arises, you will assume that this one is resolved. For example, "John, if there's another way I can help you, let me know. Otherwise, you can proceed on your own."

Before you spend time trying to eliminate a problem, assess the situation carefully. Is it really a problem, or is it a cue for you to adjust your style? It is easy to incorrectly judge someone's behavior as a problem, when it is simply different from the behavior you are expecting. For example, suppose Bob is keying ahead in the book. He's always at least a page ahead of the rest of the class. Is it a problem if Bob keys ahead in the course? If he's not disrupting others, why not let Bob work comfortably using his preferred style, while others might prefer to hear more about the topic before performing hands-on activities? Some trainers encourage learners to use their own style. And they point out places in the book where procedures are tricky, where learners might need more guidance. But before you give students that freedom, you should know their needs and styles. And you should know how to adjust your style and work with them.

In computer training courses, trainers often require all learners to follow along during class. This makes a nice, neat class where very little can go wrong. The trainer is in complete control, and the learners do just what they're told. This style is safe for the trainer because it gives the trainer maximum control over everything and everyone involved. But don't forget, this style crushes creativity, critical thinking, and the transfer of skills. Trainers fear losing control. So, they tighten the reins. Yet letting people learn at their own pace, using their own particular style of learning, is a goal every trainer should strive for. When you release the learners from your control, you give them control over their own learning. And that's what good training is all about. For more information about how to successfully help learners be responsible for their own learning, see Chapter 2, "A Logical Approach to Training."

Chapter 8

Evaluation: Effective Training and Trainers

Evaluation is the barometer of training; it measures the events of the past and present to help you forecast the future.

The best trainers believe there is always room for improvement. They work hard to solicit honest feedback. And they continually try new ways to improve their skills in such areas as presentation, design, and assessment. They perceive evaluation and feedback as a bonus. After all, if someone offered you a map showing the location of a pot of gold at the end of a rainbow, wouldn't you take it?

Why evaluate?

Before the training event, you conducted a needs assessment and designed training for individuals based on their needs and expectations. Then you prepared for the delivery of the training event. Now it's time to evaluate the training. How well did it go? Could it have been better? Were learners' needs and expectations met?

You started out with a set of objectives that you presented to the class. Did anyone add objectives to your list? Everyone agreed upon the objectives at the start of class. Now that the training is nearly over, you need to check and see if the objectives have been met. You might think that you met them all, but the person who added a particular objective might disagree. You need to resolve this before the end of class. Without evaluation, there is no measure of success. If the training was not successful, do you know why? Were the materials inappropriate? Was the trainer ineffective? Evaluations help you polish your skills as a trainer. You'll get better at assessing needs. You'll get better at designing training. And you'll get better at presenting information. But first you have to learn to use feedback to your advantage and become a star trainer. (See Chapter 5, "Preparing for Class.") Evaluation connects all the pieces in the puzzle.

Suppose your training assignment is well defined. You know the subject matter, and you know when and where the training will take place. What other information do you need to know? What else do you need to do? Consider the following:

1. Do you want to improve your skills as a trainer?

2. Are you testing a new course or product to determine whether or not to continue offering it?

3. Do you need to justify the existence of the training department?

Improving Your Skills

All of the items above are valid reasons for you to evaluate training. It is a natural progression for people to move toward personal growth. We always want to be our best. In fact, we want to be *the* best. Evaluation points out areas where you excel and areas where you need to improve. It's that yearning for success and improvement that drives people to seek feedback. Some types of feedback are difficult to receive. Keep in mind that feedback is not a personal attack; it is not a criticism of you. Instead it is constructive awareness that will help you succeed. The time to be concerned is when you find yourself not wanting to improve, not excited about your work, and just not having fun anymore. These are symptoms of burnout, which is discussed in detail in the next chapter.

Assessing Needs After Class

As a trainer, your goal is to work toward stardom—continuously— because just as a good teacher never stops learning, a good trainer never stops learning. If you ask a former teacher why he or she changed careers, the response is often that the excitement was gone. Sometimes you'll even hear the words, "I'm not learning anything anymore." To be a good trainer, you have to seek continual learning.

The feedback you receive after class can make a valuable contribution to your future training events. Routinely ask for constructive criticism. Depending on your comfort level, you can even tell learners before you start that you want as much feedback and as many suggestions as they want to give. However, don't use this event as your dry run (see Chapter 5, "Preparing for Class"). The people in your class deserve a prepared trainer. Encourage people to give feedback after class. Otherwise, they will focus on your training methods and style instead of the subject matter in the course. The benefit of asking for feedback and suggestions is twofold: you take the pressure off learners and place it on yourself, which creates a relaxed atmosphere, and you come away with things you can work on for the next training event.

Sometimes you have to beg people for feedback. The quality that sets apart star trainers from other trainers is a desire for personal growth. And that comes with confidence. During your first few training events, you might get so much feedback that you just can't handle it all. Categorize feedback into two groups: things I can do now, and things I can do later. Then prioritize the items in each group. Be careful not to overload yourself. You shouldn't expect to take care of everything before the next training event. And you'll find that some of the items will become long-term goals.

Trainers often overlook praise. Praise is just as important as critical feedback for your personal growth. It instills confidence and motivation, and helps you reach your goals. One way to make sure you notice praise is to keep a personal top ten list. This is something you can do with your supervisor. List the reasons you, instead of someone else, were hired for this job, such as sense of humor, enthusiasm, intelligence, perky attitude, and so on. Then, before each class, find time to read the contents of the list. You can make this activity part of your before-class aerobics. This simple little activity can boost your spirits and make your training event better. We often focus on what we can improve on, and forget about what we do so well.

Self-Evaluation

You can evaluate yourself every time you teach a class. There are several techniques you can use to accomplish this.

- Practice activities. Whenever possible, you should assign independent practice activities. Learners like to practice their new skills, and you can use the activities to confirm that learning has taken place.

- Questions. Rather than explaining every detail, ask learners to explain. Give them a scenario and ask them to solve a problem. As part of your setup for a concept, ask learners what they think the new concept means. Ask the group to define the concept. Then you can reinforce the concept by building on the group's definition. When you, the trainer, answer your own questions or explain the concepts, it is not apparent if learners understand. Encourage learner participation.

- Videotaping. You can observe yourself and critique your training event. And you can review the videotape many times in the future. Each time you view the tape, you might notice something else that you want to work on. You might even be able to see the learners' reactions to your presentation. Focus on an objective observation of yourself. When you find things to work on, prioritize them according to short-term and long-term goals. And remember to avoid being too critical. Don't hesitate to praise yourself for a job well done.

- Audiotaping. You can critique your presentation and focus on key elements, such as your questioning technique, the number of questions learners answered versus the number you answered, and how long you waited for learners to answer. You can also critique your setup, delivery, and follow-up methods.

- Self-evaluation form. This is a simple form that you can create. In fact, all you need is a sheet of paper. Make three columns labeled "questions," "learners," and "trainer," or other labels that work well for you. Every time you ask a question, put a check mark in the first column. Then, check column 2 or 3 based on who answers the question. This technique is very simple, and it reminds you to ask questions. It also enables you to change your technique immediately if you notice that you have few check marks in the questions column.

Peer Evaluation

Your peers are a great source of feedback. Periodically, ask another trainer to observe your training event. By using an observation form, the observer is more likely to focus on objective areas, not subjective areas. Follow the four steps below for an effective observation.

1. Data collection. You should have a trainer portfolio in which you keep data that you have collected from your self-evaluations. Include your concerns. What areas do you need to improve on?

2. Pre-observation meeting. At this meeting, share your concerns with the observer. Share the data you have collected in your portfolio. This way, the observer knows which areas you are trying to improve, and he or she can pay close attention to those areas. Tell the observer what part of the training event you want him or her to observe. Remind the observer to list no more than 2 or 3 action items.

3. Observation. The observation should last no longer than 45 minutes. To avoid disrupting the class, the observer should start at the beginning of class, or after a break. Give the observer an objective form to use. This helps the observer remain focused on the proper areas, and avoid subjective areas.

4. Evaluation conference. Be sure to schedule this meeting to occur within a few days after the training event. If you wait, you and the observer might get confused about which event was observed. Be sure to take time to read the observation prior to this meeting. This saves time and gives the trainer time to consider the information. You might also want to have a short overview meeting directly after the event to get the observer's immediate reaction to the event.

We've included the Objective Observation Analysis form that we use in our training events. You can make your own observation form using our form as a model.

Objective Observation Analysis

Name of trainer _____ Name of observer _____

Date _____ Start time _____ End time _____

Title of class _____ Additional facilitator present: Yes ___ No___
Number of lessons _____
Number of topics _____
Number of tasks _____

I. Scheduling

Timing. The trainer was on the following tasks at the following 5-minute intervals.

Time	Task #	Time	Task #

Comments _____
_____

Time on task. The learners' screens match the trainer's screen at the time of the observation. Measurement is expressed as a percent in units of on task/off task every 5 minutes.

Number of learners _____   Number of screens on task

Comments _____
_____

Correct start/stop times. Did the trainer start and stop on time? Yes ___ No___.
If no, how many minutes off schedule, using 5-minute increments? (Peak performance is within 5 minutes.)

Comments _____
_____
_____
_____

Objective Observation Analysis

II. Linking

Questions asked by the trainer. When the trainer asks a question, how often does the following happen? a) learners answer, b) trainer prompts learners for the answer, or c) trainer provides the answer. Did the trainer wait a recommended nine seconds for a response? Par is achieved when learners answer 80% of the questions.

Column 1 should equal the combined total of columns 2 and 3. Column 4 is completed only if the learner provides the answer.

1. Trainer asked a question (✓)	2. Learner answered (✓)	3. Trainer answered (✓)	4. Wait/pause time (9 seconds)

Comments _____

_____

_____

Questions asked by learners. The learners ask a question and the trainer responds.

1. Learner asked a question (✓)	2. Trainer repeated the question (✓)	3. Trainer answered the question (✓)

Columns 1, 2, and 3 should have equal numbers of checkmarks.

Comments _____

_____

_____

Eye contact. With how many learners did the trainer attempt to make eye contact? (Par is 80%.) Observe at predetermined intervals.

Diagram of Classroom:

Objective Observation Analysis

III. Use of Manual

Page references and transitions. In one lesson, the trainer gave adequate page references and transitions between topics. (The minimum recommendation is one reference and transition for each topic in a lesson.)

	Topic A	Topic B	Topic C	Topic D	Topic E
Setup and/or follow-up transitions					
Page references					

Comments _____
_____
_____

Trainer preparation. Check areas observed and the topics in which the areas are taught.

	Topic A	Topic B	Topic C	Topic D	Topic E
Floating, lengthy pauses					
Page references					
Knowledge of material					

Comments _____
_____
_____

Successful completion of independent tasks. Learners independently completed an assigned task according to the trainer's directions. Measurement is expressed in percentage. (Par is 90%.)

Total number of learners ____   Number of successful completions of task

Comments_____
_____
_____
_____

101

Objective Observation Analysis

IV. Recommended Action Items

Action items

1. _____
   _____
   _____
   _____
   _____
   _____
   _____
   _____

2. _____
   _____
   _____
   _____
   _____
   _____
   _____
   _____
   _____

3. _____
   _____
   _____
   _____
   _____
   _____
   _____
   _____

Trainer's Signature _____   Date _____

Observer's Signature _____   Date _____

Testing New Courses and Products

Development of a new product or course includes testing. Are the benefits of the new product or course greater than its costs? If not, perhaps it should be discontinued. Evaluation is the process by which you determine value. The training department is like a business within the organization. As such it needs to monitor its expenditures and increase its revenues. Evaluation provides information that enables a training department to make sound judgments and decisions about its services.

Justifying Training

Fearing what will happen if you cannot justify the existence of your training department is plenty of reason for listing evaluation high on your priority list. And maintaining an effective evaluation process becomes more and more important every day. Evaluation determines the effectiveness of training. It tells you which systems are working and which are not. Similar to a gauge, its indicators alert you when there is a malfunction. Did the people taking the course learn? What went right? What went wrong? What could have been better? Each question is based on the assumption that there is always room for improvement. Consider the following questions to determine how training can be improved:

- Does the subject matter of the course meet the needs of the learners?

- Is the trainer qualified to teach the course?

- Is the trainer using effective methods to accomplish the desired results?

- Are the training facilities adequate?

- Does the schedule meet the needs of the learners?

- Are teaching aids used appropriately?

- Did the training event proceed smoothly?

- Are there additional factors that might improve the training?

Today's businesses are more fast-paced than ever. In a world where strict accountability is the norm, individual departments are forced to demonstrate their worth on a continuing basis. Training departments are often seen as fluff, a benefit offered during prosperous times. At the first sight of economic hardship, training diminishes and often disappears altogether. Yet training should play an important role in maintaining a strong business. During economic stress, proper training can boost the recovery rate. When people are losing their jobs, and being labeled as "not having the skills for the new direction of the company," businesses should rely on their training departments to train and retrain employees for upcoming changes.

Current employees have spent years with the company and know their products. They have built company loyalty and support. It takes years to develop product knowledge and company culture. Skills often take only months to develop, starting with training and then practice. Therefore, it is often more cost-effective to retrain current employees than to hire new employees who might have the new skills, but not the product knowledge, an understanding of the company culture, or company loyalty and support. Employees who "know the business" can help an organization prosper. It takes an extended period of time to build an identity with the culture of an organization. The training department is a company's support department—it goes to work quickly to make a smooth transition from the company's direction today to its direction for tomorrow. Dedicated employees are valuable resources. They have a personal stake in the company, and they want it to succeed.

It is in the best interest of a training department to continually justify its existence. If you sit passively and assume that management will continue to favorably consider the value of training, your department is a sitting duck. You don't know if today's management will be tomorrow's management, and you don't know if today's values will be tomorrow's values. After all, how do you suppose training departments fell into a category called "fluff" in the first place? They were not asked to justify their existence and they did not. Training was seen by many as a nice-to-have company benefit. Cost was never questioned. Yet, when hard economic times hit, training was decreased if not eliminated altogether, which suggests that cost is a hidden factor, important only during hard times. Senior management continually investigates ways to save and make money. If there is no apparent justification for a department, what is the purpose for its existence? Management must, at any given time, be able to quickly defend the existence of any department based on its benefits in terms of dollars and cents.

Kirkpatrick's Four Levels of Evaluation

In his quest to provide a simple, practical, four-level approach for evaluating training, Dr. Donald Kirkpatrick of the University of Wisconsin designed a sequence of ways to evaluate programs:

> **Level 1: Reaction.** What was the reaction of the learners? Put your customer service skills to work. Think of the people in your training events as customers, whether you are training people from your organization or people from an outside company. Every learner deserves the best training available.

Level 2: Learning. Did the learners change their attitudes, improve their knowledge, or increase their skills as a result of the training? It is important to evaluate learning because the results indicate whether or not a behavioral change is expected.

Level 3: Behavior. To what extent did the actions of learners change? According to Kirkpatrick, some trainers make the serious mistake of bypassing levels 1 and 2 and immediately measuring changes in behavior. He argues that this is risky. Suppose no change in behavior is discovered. Is it reasonable to conclude that the training was ineffective and should be discontinued? Reaction might have been favorable, and the objectives might have been met. But for some other reason, behavior might not have changed and production might not have increased after training. Dr. Kirkpatrick offers four conditions that must be met if change is to occur:

1. The learner must have a desire to change.

2. The learner must know what to do and how to do it.

3. The learner must work in the right climate.

4. The learner must be rewarded for changing.

For conditions 1 and 2 to be met, the training event must create a positive attitude in learners toward the desired change, and the necessary knowledge and skills must be taught. The third condition is determined by the learner's supervisor. If the learner embraces training, but the supervisor does not support the training by letting the learner use his or her new skills, then the climate is not right. The fourth condition requires reward. If there is no incentive for the learner, then why make an effort to learn? And if these requirements are not met, there will be no change and the learner will not accept responsibility for the training, because it does not hold value.

Level 4: Results. As a result of training, did production increase, did quality improve, did costs decrease? These are questions that describe the final results. They circle back to the reasons for the training in the first place. The objectives for the training event were based on needs, which come into play again as you analyze the results of the training event. Needs do not directly produce tangible results, such as increased productivity, which can be measured in dollars and cents. Needs enable you to identify objectives and set the direction for the training event. For example, training in time management and decision-making will not directly increase productivity. Yet by learning skills in these areas, learners can become more efficient and make sound decisions, which in turn causes productivity to increase.

Each level is more complex than the previous level. Training should begin with a need and a desired outcome. Then decide what behaviors are required to meet that need and desired outcome. One common problem in organizations is not sharing information. Training in this case should include why sharing information is important, when information should be shared, and how to properly share information. Training should also include learning to work as teams, recognizing the company goal, and staying focused on individual work as it pertains to the big picture. The desired results are sharing information and learning to work together, not increasing productivity. This, in turn, yields increased productivity.

Implementing the Four Levels of Evaluation

When you implement the four levels of evaluation, attend to each level in order. The reason, as explained in the previous section, is to avoid

107

drawing incorrect conclusions. By evaluating reaction and learning first, you can determine whether a lack of change is the result of an ineffective training program, a poor job climate, or a lack of incentive. If you start with Level 3, Behavior, and you decide that the training was ineffective, you might identify an incorrect reason for the lack of change.

Part of implementation is designing an effective evaluation form. If your organization does not specify a particular form, you might choose to order forms that meet your needs, or you can design your own form. There are several styles that you can use, but the ideal form provides the maximum amount of information and requires a minimum amount of time. Also include an area on your form where learners can add comments and suggestions.

Implementation begins with Level 1, Reaction. Although it is difficult to please everyone, in every way, and every time, your standards should be high. Remember, the learners are your customers. Read all of the comments and suggestions and look for ideas about ways to improve. Often the way you perceive yourself is not the same as how others perceive you. And you want to please the customer. But that doesn't mean that one negative reaction out of 25 warrants a change in your style. It is an awareness. You should decide ahead of time what type and percentage of negative reaction warrants change.

Level 2, Learning, tests the knowledge, skills, and attitudes that learners are required to perform by the end of the training event. A post-class assessment can identify skill levels after class. A pre-class assessment provides a basis for comparison.

Level 3, Behavior, requires statistical research and a sophisticated evaluation form. Unless you are skilled in the area of statistical analysis, you might want to rely on an expert to develop this part of the evaluation form. Did the training change the behavior of the learners? If so, to what extent did the training change their behavior?

Level 4, Results, also requires statistical research. What has occurred as a result of the training? Has production or quality improved? Have costs decreased? The results you are looking for should match the initial reasons for the training.

Guidelines to Check the Effectiveness of Training

You can design your own personal guidelines to check the effectiveness of your training events. Or you can use the checklist provided here. This checklist assumes that training has been identified as the solution to a need.

1. Conduct a needs assessment to determine what type of training is appropriate.

2. Based on the identified need, set the objectives.

3. Based on the objectives, determine the appropriate content.

4. Decide what group needs the training.

5. Map out the training schedule.

6. Select appropriate facilities.

7. Select appropriate trainers.

8. Select appropriate materials.

9. Coordinate the training.

10. Evaluate the training.

Chapter 9

The Burnout Blues

Similar to the flu, burnout leaves you drained of
your energy and feeling out of sorts.

You go to bed tired. And you wake up in the morning still feeling tired.
You don't have any interest or energy to do anything. Even a vacation
sounds like too much work. If these symptoms are familiar to you, you
might be experiencing burnout.

Burnout doesn't happen overnight. There are warning signs that tell you
when something is wrong. And if you attend to burnout early, there is a
cure. A severe case of burnout can result in major depression.
Remember, having burnout symptoms doesn't mean you have burnout.
It simply means that you are showing signs of burnout. Now is the time
to address the symptoms, while you can still avoid burnout.

It is often difficult to attend to the symptoms of burnout because part of
burnout is denial. Rather than accepting responsibility for our dilemma,
we often refuse to admit that *we* made the choices that caused our
dilemma. Instead, we feel victimized by everyone and everything. "The
company isn't giving me what I need." "The other trainers aren't
supporting me." "My supervisor is overloading me." "I don't have time
to get my job done." "I don't even have time to eat lunch." We are not
able to see that our choices are directly linked to our dilemma. And we
don't believe we have options. Yet, *we* made the decision to accept more

work than we could handle. And *we* decided to work instead of eating lunch.

Treating burnout symptoms is an on-going process because burnout symptoms typically flare up again from time to time. It might start with a last-minute project that requires you to work additional hours. Once you are in a fast-paced lifestyle, it's difficult to get back to a normal pace. The next thing you know, almost every project is a rush, requiring additional hours. The key to conquering burnout is to be aware of the signs, acknowledge the symptoms when they exist, and take care of them right away.

Five Steps to Managing Stress and Avoiding Burnout

Managing stress is an on-going process. Begin by identifying where the stress is coming from.

1. Awareness. You need to monitor your stress at all times. A certain amount of stress is healthy and stimulating. But when you find yourself depressed for long periods of time, and consistently not feeling well, your stress is no longer healthy and stimulating. Left unchecked, stress can lead to burnout.

2. Analysis. What is causing your stress? Is it related to problems inside the classroom, such as individuals or peers? Or is it related to problems outside the classroom, such as your preparation techniques? Often, you can get a clearer picture of what is wrong if you ask another person to help you with your analysis. Others often see what we overlook. On paper, make a list of the things that are causing your stress. Categorize things you can change or update and things you cannot change.

3.   Strategies. After you identify the possible causes of your stress, list some ways to end or limit your stress. For each item on your list, provide some ideas to alleviate the problem. You might find that you need to use checklists more often, or you might need to re-evaluate your preparation techniques. Or you might find that you need to take more vacations from your work, and form support groups where you can share ideas and experiences with other trainers.

4.   Implementation. Don't try to change everything at once. Start with the most important items on your list. And remember, improvement takes time. Don't expect everything to be better after the first change you make.

5.   Reflection. After you implement your strategies, measure your stress level. Are there measurable changes that indicate improvement? If so, continue your strategies. If you cannot observe an improvement, review your analysis and your strategies. Brainstorm for ideas and make appropriate changes.

As a trainer, you should be realistic about your career. Always have a goal in mind. It doesn't have to be a major goal. It might be as simple as learning and teaching a new course every six months. Or you might get involved in a management role or advisory group for your organization. These ideas can fill gaps in your job and make your career as a trainer more fulfilling.

In her book, *You Don't Have To Go Home From Work Exhausted!*, Ann McGee-Cooper talks about three profiles that lead to burnout: perfectionism, "fast-lane" living, and the superhuman syndrome. She claims that each profile is linked to high performance. We compete to be the best, we race to be the fastest, we like to be the hero.

Perfectionism

The perfectionist strives to be perfect in every way. He or she has a reputation of always being right, reliable, and exceptional. The perfectionist works harder and harder at being perfect, and gets less and less satisfaction from his or her efforts. This behavior drains the energy of the perfectionist, which can lead to burnout.

If you identify with the perfectionist, try spending time at the end of each day to focus on the events of your day. Think about each task that you did well. You probably do a lot of tasks well every day. Then think about the things that didn't go well. Did you learn from them? If you can come up with at least one thing you learned from a failed task, then it was a good experience. McGee-Cooper also suggests doing something imperfectly each day. She suggests that this enables perfectionists to learn to accept initial feelings of awkwardness and insecurity, and to enjoy the challenge and satisfaction of trying new things.

Living in the Fast Lane

Fast-lane behavior means beating everyone to the prize. People who live in the fast lane are highly productive and tend to be frequently promoted. They are always on the go, with an eye toward what lies ahead. But they have a tendency to go for quick fixes and short-term solutions, which often affect long-term results negatively.

Our society encourages and rewards high-speed performance. We often measure performance in terms of speed. We have no patience for slow traffic or slow computers. We demand fast food and high-speed fax machines. In essence, fast is never fast enough. Because everything around us is fast-paced, we easily slip into life in the fast lane. And we start at a very early age. Parents compare the ages at which their children start to walk. They brag about how early Johnny learned to read. And they're quick to enroll their children in nursery school to keep pace with the other children.

If you find yourself living in the fast lane, try scheduling your projects with more balance. Separate the projects that leave you feeling pressured and fatigued from the projects that leave you feeling stimulated and enthusiastic. When you are working on a project that is stressful, take time out to enjoy a visit with someone or do something relaxing. Schedule your time so that you work on the stressful project during your most energetic times of the day. This way, you can minimize your stress and maximize your performance.

Superhuman Syndrome

You can do anything. You're everybody's hero. The problem is you have no time for yourself. And you don't feel that you have worth unless you are coming to the aid of others or performing miraculous feats. Does this sound like you?

Instead of always having the answer, try listening to other people. Give them an opportunity to provide the right answer. Remember, there are other people who are just as qualified as you. If you truly believe that you are the only person who can resolve a specific set of problems, then it is time for you to teach others the skills you are using to resolve problems. Then stand back and let them handle a problem. It might be frustrating at first for you to let this happen, but in time others will become more proficient at resolving problems. And you will have less pressure and desire to be superhuman.

Everyone has activities that he or she enjoys. As a superhuman, you've been too busy pleasing everyone else to take time for your own pleasures. Now is the time to do some of those activities, as you limit your availability to others. Give your personal needs additional weight on your priority list.

Curing Burnout

Knowing and facing the symptoms of burnout can help you reach a
balance in your life. Start by building up your energy to a level that you
are comfortable with. Ann McGee-Cooper researched at least twelve key
lifestyle factors that affect energy. Some of those factors are listed below.
(All of you conceptual thinkers are probably itching to know which ones
are *not* listed below.) As you consider each area, keep in mind that you
might be able to add more areas, and that everyone has an energy level
that is particular to his or her needs.

- Proper rest is important to your energy level. Sometimes
  additional sleep revitalizes us. Other times, play and
  pleasure renew us more than sleep. McGee-Cooper claims
  that the secret is to listen to your body. Rest if you feel
  tired. Some people require just a few hours' sleep, while
  others need more than eight hours every night. And her
  second secret is to enjoy work and play, with equal
  commitment to both.

- The food you eat and the beverages you drink affect your
  energy. We all know that too much coffee has a negative
  effect on your body's metabolism and your heartbeat. And
  coffee and tea are said to flush out significant chemicals
  that are necessary in your body. More and more people are
  catching on to the trend of drinking water, which we all
  know is good for us. If you keep a full glass of fresh water
  on your desk at all times, you might be surprised at how
  much of it you will drink. Maybe it's just having something
  in your cup that matters, not necessarily what is in your
  cup. Try it and see.

- Do you get enough exercise? For many of us, mental
  aerobics is as far as we get. We think about exercising and
  we even make resolutions about getting more exercise. So
  why not try something fun. Arrange time to take a brisk
  walk with a group of people that you enjoy. Start walking

several times a week or, better yet, daily. Most people are full of conversation. You'll benefit from the social time with friends, and you'll be exercising, too. By the end of your walk, you'll all be arranging your next outing.

- Most people require some time alone. If you are one of those people, make sure you give yourself the time you need. It can increase your energy level and your performance level.

- What do you do to have fun? And when is the best time to have fun? As children, we learned to finish our work first, and then have fun. As adults, we need to schedule our fun differently. In most cases, there is no end to our work. So if you wait until you finish your work, you'll never have fun. Instead, take frequent fun breaks. Learn to leave your work at the office and enjoy your weekend. Don't let it drain you of your energy. Having fun refreshes you and helps you perform better.

- Have you ever noticed how it often takes a family emergency to convince you that you need to spend more time with your family? Well, if this is you, make a list of your priorities. When you schedule your activities, be sure to include personal time for your family and other priorities (fun, exercise, time alone). If you don't plan time for them, you might not have or take time for them. And most of us will agree that our family is the most important part of our lives.

- Hobbies aren't just for kids. But many people leave their hobbies behind when they settle into adulthood. Your hobby is part of what defines you; it's part of your identity. And the more time you spend on work, the less time you have for yourself. Hobbies become part of your energy-building tools, just like exercise, good food, sleep, time alone, family, and fun.

- Are you like many people who let their vacation time build up, and then never use it because they don't have time? Do you think that no one else can take care of your work while you're away? Many people think that the business can't function without them. If this describes you, try to find ways to share your abilities with others. Examine your priority list. Move some personal joys to the top of the list.

These are all healthy choices for you. No one but you can make your choices. Beyond building immediate energy, these choices give you a sense of purpose in your life. As you look back over the key lifestyle factors listed above, you might see yourself described in several styles. And you might say that you don't exercise, spend time alone, or take vacations because you don't have time. But time is only an excuse. The choice is still yours. You would probably be amazed at the energy you spend (or waste) avoiding your opportunities. If you'd like to read more about balancing your life with joy and energy, a good way to start is by reading *You Don't Have To Go Home From Work Exhausted!* by Ann McGee-Cooper.

Analogies for Computer Training

Though analogy is misleading, it is the least misleading thing we have.

—Samuel Butler, *Notebooks*, "Music, Pictures and Books: Thought and Word."

An analogy is a comparison based on similarities. The analogies provided here are specific to computer training. You can use these analogies to explain concepts in such areas as databases, file management, graphics, operating systems, spreadsheets, word processing, and networking.

By using analogies to relate a new concept to a familiar concept, you can help people to learn and understand the new concept. Keep in mind that analogies do not provide technical information. They serve as a bridge between the familiar and the unfamiliar. Once learners make that connection, they are ready to learn the new concept.

We cannot guarantee that you will be successful with every analogy, so we have provided an assortment from which you can choose. Because learners typically have a wide range of skill levels, we suggest that you use more than one analogy to explain a particular concept. Ideas that are familiar to some students might not be familiar to others. By using more than one analogy, you can help more people make the connection to the new concept.

Databases

A database is like a collection of index cards. There is one card for each item and its information. To access that information, you check the index card and then search for the information you want.

A database is like a refrigerator. Just as a refrigerator holds a collection of cold foods, a database holds a collection of related information.

A database is like a telephone book. Entries in the telephone book are sorted alphabetically. To find a telephone number, you look up the name of the person or organization you want to call.

Creating a database is like building a house. First, you plan the database on paper, just as you plan the house on blueprints. Then you create the database structure, just as you build the house. Next, you enter data into the table, just as you move furniture into the house. Finally, after testing the database, you identify problems and modify the database, just as you rearrange the dishes in the cupboards and the furniture in the rooms. You would not build the house without first planning, because it is difficult to change the house after it is built. The same is true for a database.

Deleting records from a database is like cutting down trees in a forest. Just as you mark the trees before you cut them down, you mark the records before you delete them.

Database objects are like the limbs on your body. Reports, forms, and indexes are attached to the main body, or database. They cannot exist without the database. Likewise, your arms and legs won't work if they aren't attached to your body.

The Control Center is like the bridge of a ship. From the bridge, you perform the major tasks for a ship. Likewise, from the Control Center, you perform the major tasks for a database.

A table is like a single family; a database is like a family reunion. At a family reunion, many families with a common bond join together. Just as families are linked by relatives, database tables are linked by key fields.

Linking tables is like cross-referencing directories. If you have identification information in the address table, and parking lot information in the parking lot table, you can link the tables and find information that pertains to both tables easily and quickly.

Linking tables through a common field is like linking two otherwise unrelated people through a common relative. James and Max are brothers-in-law, related to each other through Mary, who is James' wife and Max's sister. If Mary were not married to James, then Max and James would not be related.

A deleted table is like a trash bin. Both are set aside for pickup. And like the trash, deleted records can be recycled.

A lookup table is like a library. You use a library to look up information. You use a lookup table to look up data stored in another table. To define a lookup, you use only the first field in the lookup table. Therefore, the data you want to look up must be stored in the first field of the lookup table *and* it must be the same field type and size. This is like saying that the information at the library must be found on the first floor *and* it must be in the same language as the article you are writing.

An AS operator is like a nickname. Your friend's name is Robert, but you call him Bob. Likewise, the calculated field is calculating Hours*Pay Rate, but you refer to that field as Gross Pay.

Memo fields are like self-stick notes. Just as you can place a self-stick note in a strategic place to serve as a reminder, you can place a memo field in a record to hold an important notation.

Validity checks are like proofreaders. They compare entries to agreed-upon conventions.

Reporting in databases is like filtering coffee. Just as you filter coffee to separate the grounds from the liquid, reporting filters data to allow only the data you want to see and work with.

A query form is like a catalog order form. Just as you provide item numbers, quantity, sizes, and colors when ordering merchandise from a catalog, you provide information for the various fields on a query form. When you press [F2], Paradox searches the database for the information you requested. The results of the query are in the ANSWER table.

Using an OR condition is like crossing the border into another country. Suppose the country has two borders that allow entry; each border has a guard. If one guard refuses you entry into the country, you can try the second guard. An OR condition appears on two rows of the query form. In order for a record to appear in the ANSWER table, it must meet the value specified in one of the rows. If a record does not meet the value specified in the first row of the query form, you can try the value specified in the second row.

Using an AND condition is like crossing the border into another country. Just as you have one border with two checkpoints to gain entrance into a country, the AND condition has one row in a query form. A record must match the two values specified in order to be part of the ANSWER table.

AND and OR conditions are like toll booths on a highway. Just as you must pay a toll to travel on a toll road, you must meet specific criteria in AND and OR conditions. The toll booth is usually a single gate, although there can be a second row of gates. In a spreadsheet, the data, upon reaching a logical condition (toll booth), must meet specific criteria in order to proceed (to the next toll booth). The first booth might be called "first name," the second might be called "last name," the third might be called "city of residence," and so on. If at any point during the sequence you are unable to pay the toll (the record does not meet the criteria), you must turn around and go back.

Using AND and OR conditions is like apartment hunting. If you want an apartment that has two bedrooms *AND* a monthly rent under $500, you search for both conditions. If you want an apartment that has two bedrooms *OR* a monthly rent under $500, you need to meet only one condition. Therefore, OR conditions are easier to meet.

File management

The hard disk is like a parking lot. Just as the parking lot is divided into parking spaces, defined by lines, the hard disk is divided into spaces, defined by sectors.

Memory is like liquid in a measuring cup. When you turn off the power to the computer, the memory cup is emptied. When you turn on the computer, the operating system is copied from the hard disk into the memory cup.

Menus are like doors in a corridor. Just as each door brings you to a new area or room, each menu choice brings you to a new area of the menu called a submenu.

Hardware is like office equipment; software is like the people who operate the equipment. Just as people use office equipment to accomplish tasks, computers use software to accomplish tasks.

A subdirectory is like a file drawer. Just as you store paper files in a file drawer, you store computer files in a subdirectory.

A shared directory is like a public library. Just as a public library shares books and other information with cardholders, a shared directory shares files with members of the workgroup.

The computer screen is like an office desktop. Just as the top of your desk contains papers, pencils, and other objects that help you perform your work, the Desktop contains objects that help you perform your work. You can arrange the objects on your desk, and you can arrange the objects on your Desktop.

The computer filing system is like an office filing system. Storing computer information is like storing paper documents in a filing cabinet that has several drawers.

- **A disk is like a drawer in the filing cabinet.** Within a filing-cabinet drawer, you can find hanging folders, manila folders, and pieces of paper.

- **A directory that contains other directories is like a hanging folder which contains manila folders.**

- **A directory that contains related files is like a manila folder that contains pieces of paper that contain related information.**

- **Files are like the pieces of paper in the folder.**

A directory tree is like a family tree. Just as the trunk of the tree is the first generation of parents, the root directory is the parent directory for the subdirectories. Each directory, or child, can become a parent to the next generation or subdirectory.

A path is like an organization chart. Just as authority flows from the top person on the chart to the bottom person on the chart, a path lists directories from the root directory to the destination directory or file.

The windows on your screen are like windows in your house. Just as a window in your house lets you see what is inside, the window on your screen lets you see what is inside.

Several windows on your Desktop are like several papers stacked on your desk. Just as a stack of papers on your desk has one paper on top, a stack of windows on your Desktop has one window on top. And just as you can move a paper to the top of the stack, you can select or open a window to move that window to the top.

The windows on your Desktop are like a deck of cards. You can stack them so that only the top one is visible, or you can arrange them so that part of each one is showing.

Learning to use the mouse is like learning to drive a car. Both seem difficult at first, but they become easier with practice.

A formatted cell is like a person wearing sunglasses and a hat. Although the sunglasses and hat change the appearance, the person remains the same. Also, the sunglasses and the hat can be removed.

Changing Desktop settings is like rearranging the furniture in your home. When you rearrange the furniture, you change the appearance of the room. The furniture is the same. When you rearrange the Desktop, you change its appearance, but the objects remain the same.

Saving a file on disk is like recording a television program on a videotape. Just as the contents of the screen are stored in a permanent location for future use, the recorded television program is saved on a videotape.

A program group is like a card catalog in a library. Just as a card catalog provides the title, author, and other information for a book, a program group provides the name, location, and executable command for a program.

A program item is like a menu item in a restaurant. Just as a menu item is a text representation of food that a restaurant serves, a program item is a graphic representation of a file name.

A Task List is like a shopping list. Just as your shopping list contains items you need to buy, the Task List contains tasks you need to accomplish.

A deleted folder is like a waste basket. If you throw away an important piece of paper, you can retrieve it from the waste basket. If you erase a message, you can retrieve it from the deleted folder. After you take the garbage to the dump, you cannot retrieve it. After you exit the program, the deleted folder is emptied and you cannot retrieve it.

Splitting a worksheet window into panes is like adding another window to your house. By adding a window to a house, you can view more of the inside of the house. By splitting the worksheet window, you can create multiple panes, which enable you to view different areas of the same worksheet.

Tiled windows are like floor tiles. Just as floor tiles are arranged in a flat side-by-side pattern on the floor, window tiles are arranged on the screen in a flat side-by-side pattern.

Cascaded windows are like a waterfall. Windows are stacked neatly on the Desktop in an overlapping fashion. They flow from one to another like a waterfall.

The Control Panel is like a dashboard in a car. Just as the dashboard has a steering wheel, turn signals, speedometer, and gauges that enable you to operate the car, the Control Panel has controls that enable you to operate a personal computer. And just as you can adjust the components of the dashboard, you can adjust the features in the Control Panel.

The main menu is like a lobby of an office building with many office doors. You choose which doors (main menu items) to open depending on what you intend to do. Each office (menu item) contains staff members (submenus) that perform specific tasks.

A read-only file is like a monitor and keyboard secured under a piece of glass. Although you can see the information, you cannot access it.

A wildcard is like a joker. Just as the joker in a game of cards generally can be used to represent any card, the question mark wildcard can be used to represent any character in a file name.

Macros are like buttons on a radio. Just as you press a radio button to hear a specific radio station, you set a macro to perform a specific task.

A macro is like a scroll of music. Just as a scroll of music is a recorded series of keystrokes for the piano, a macro is a recorded sequence of keystrokes and commands.

Networking

Assigning drive mappings is like setting the batting order on a baseball team. Just as the manager establishes the batting order he or she prefers, the drive mappings can be mapped any way and changed.

A team roster is like a set of drive mappings. Just as a team is limited in the number of players it can support, the number of drive mappings is limited. Team members (drive mappings) can change, but the number of team members (drives) must remain the same.

A logical drive is like a nickname. Just as you can use the name Bob to represent the full name Robert, you can assign a logical drive to represent a full path.

Choosing the right events when adding code is like writing directions for someone. Just as you need directions to complete a journey, you need the right events when adding code.

Surfing the internet is like cruising an expressway. Both have many options.

Browsers are like custom maps. They make it easy for you to find your way.

A read-only file is like a restaurant menu posted on the restaurant window. You can see the items on the menu, but you cannot order from there.

The Program Manager is like a set of dresser drawers; icons are like drawers. If you want something from the middle drawer, you don't remove the drawer. Instead you open the middle drawer and get what you want.

Minimizing a group in Program Manager is like closing a dresser drawer.

Comparing 4 Megabytes of RAM to 12 Megabytes of RAM is like comparing the size of a student's desk to the size of the President's desk.

The GUI interface on a computer is like a universal sign. Just as a picture of a fork, knife, and spoon is used to indicate food, pictures are used to indicate features and choices on a computer.

Embedded objects are like drive-through bank services. Just as you reach out your car window to use the bank services, you can use an embedded object's program from within another program.

A macro recorder is like a video recorder. Just as you can record information on a video recorder, you can record procedures that you perform in a macro.

The printer driver is like a language interpreter. Just as a language interpreter translates spoken words into another language, the printer driver translates the language of a data file into a form that the printer can understand.

The print queue is like a line of customers at the store. Just as the people in line are ready to check out, the files in the print queue are ready to be printed.

Cell referencing is like playing Bingo. The location of the cell or Bingo callout depends on the row and column.

Safeguarding your worksheet is like engaging the lock on your door. When the door (worksheet) is unlocked, you can open it and change what is inside. When the door (worksheet) is locked, you cannot open it. Everything inside is protected.

Links are like handcuffs. What happens to one component affects the other. If two people are handcuffed together, and one moves to the left, the other must also move to the left.

Compressing a file is like photocopying a document at a size less than 100%. Just as the entire document is printed at a reduced size, the file takes up less space.

Loading graph settings into memory is like remodeling a house. The old material is cleared away and the new material is installed. When graph settings are loaded into memory, the default settings are cleared away and the new settings take effect.

Associating files and programs is like building a bridge. Both provide quick access to something. Removing the bridge (the association) does not remove the island (program), but it makes it more difficult to get to the island.

Adding a reminder in Schedule+ is like setting an alarm clock. Just as you set your alarm clock to wake you up at a specified time, you set a reminder so that you are not late for appointments or meetings.

Using a place holder when you change directories is like using a bookmark when you read a book. Just as you use a bookmark if you are interrupted while reading a book, you use a place holder to mark your place if you change directories. That way, every time you move to that directory, you can find where you were last working.

Chat is like a telephone. In both cases, one person calls another; they have a conversation and then hang up when they are finished.

Composing a document in Lotus Notes is like building a house. Just as cement blocks provide the foundation for a house, the form provides the foundation for the Notes document.

A DocLink is like a drive-up service at a bank. The drive-up window connects you to the teller so you don't have to park your car and walk into the bank. Likewise, a DocLink connects two Notes documents so you don't have to return to the workspace to add a database.

A logon password is like a sentry at a gate. Just as a sentry monitors the passage of people through a gate, a logon password monitors access to workgroup resources.

A password is like a key. Just as a key opens a locked door, a password enables you to access restricted information.

Creating a mail message is like writing a letter. You enter your message in the message area, address the message using the To text box, and send the message using the Send button.

Forwarding a message is like making copies of information. Just as you make paper copies for distribution, you can distribute electronic copies.

ASCII is like a language, a universal language that most programs can interpret and understand. Although there are different dialects in England, everyone understands the basic English language. And computer programs are different, although they all use a universal, or basic, language.

The left side of the File Manager screen is like the spine of a book; the right side is like the contents of the book. To see what is inside the book, click on the contents on the right side.

Graphics

Using the mouse to draw objects is like using a pen and paper. The mouse is your pen, and the screen is a piece of paper.

A shadow object is like a reflection in the mirror. Just as the reflection in the mirror does not exist without the presence of the object, a shadow object does not exist without the presence of the original object.

Using magnification is like painting a picture. Just as an artist might use a wide brush to create the background and a thin brush to create the foreground, you might use a large view and large tools to create the overall scheme for the graphic.

The background on a slide is like company stationery. Just as the company name, phone number, and logo appear on each piece of stationery, the presentation style contains a background that appears on each slide, which can be changed and applied to one or more slides.

Creating an overlay chart is like placing one overhead transparency on top of another. The individual overheads combine to form an all-inclusive overhead for projection on the screen.

Operating systems

An operating system is like an air-traffic control operator. Just as the air-traffic control operator controls the operations between the pilots and the ground crews, the operating system controls the operations between the application software and the hardware. Each keystroke is intercepted by the operating system and sent to the application program.

DOS is like a traffic cop. Just as a traffic cop controls traffic, DOS maintains the flow of events within your computer.

DOS is like a human's brain. Just as your body functions according to messages received from the brain, the computer operates according to messages received by DOS.

DOS is like a comfortable old couch; Windows is like a slipcover on a couch. The slipcover makes the couch look better, but it is still the same couch. Windows makes DOS look better, but it is still the same DOS. The commands for DOS are still available at the prompt.

Group icons are like shoe boxes filled with treasures. Just as you open the lid to see what is inside the shoe box, you double-click on the icon to find out what is inside.

The hard disk is like a hotel; the root of the directory is like the lobby. From the lobby (root) you can look at a directory listing and move through halls and corridors (directories) to new locations on the disk.

The hard disk is like a filing cabinet where you store information. Each drawer is a directory. Just as the folders in the drawers contain documents, subdirectories within directories contain files.

Disks are like measuring cups. The amount of liquid a cup holds depends on its size (small, medium, or large). The amount of data you can place on a disk depends on its size, or its capacity.

Disks are like audio-cassette tapes; they have varying capacities. The number of songs the tape can hold on each side depends on the length of the songs and the capacity of the tape; for instance, 30, 60, or 90 minutes.

A formatted disk is like lined paper. Just as lines on paper divide the paper into usable areas so that your words are straight across the page, "lines" on a formatted disk divide the disk space for storage.

An unformatted disk is like a parking lot without lines. Just as lines on a parking lot indicate where to park cars, formatting on a disk indicates where to place files.

RAM is like the short-term memory in your brain; disk storage is like long-term memory. The text on your screen is in short-term memory. If you want to be able to retrieve the text later, you can move the text to long-term memory by saving it on disk. Then you will be able to retrieve your work later.

The OS/2 Workplace Shell is like a theater set. The theater set provides a backdrop and covers behind-the-scenes events. OS/2 provides a working environment and covers the inner workings of the computer. In both cases, you cannot see what is happening behind the scenes. In the theater, the director oversees the performance. In OS/2, you are the director; you supervise its operation.

On-line information is like a printed reference manual. It is always available. You can access it while you are working, without interrupting your work flow. Depending on the resource you use, most items are cross-referenced so that related information is available.

The System Editor program is like an electronic typewriter. The System Editor enables you to create and revise documents before you print them on paper.

The Shredder object is like a garbage can. Both are used to dispose of objects that are no longer needed. When you drag an object to the Shredder and then let go, the object is dropped into the garbage can.

DDE is like a pager. A pager enables you to easily contact others; it also enables others to contact you. DDE keeps information in one place and accessible to other locations by establishing links.

Multi-tasking is like being an efficient hotel telephone operator. Just as the telephone operator switches back and forth between calls, you multi-task by switching back and forth between tasks.

Database indexes are like off-duty firefighters. Although they are always ready for action, they don't start working until you call them.

Spreadsheets

An electronic worksheet (or spreadsheet) is like an accountant's ledger sheet. Both sheets are used for numeric analysis, and both are defined by columns and rows. When you change a number on the ledger paper, you have to change every number that is affected. But when you change a number on the electronic worksheet, it automatically updates all numbers that are affected.

The cell pointer is like a pencil. Both are used to enter information into the worksheet.

Resetting sort settings is like wiping the board clean. After you clean the board or reset the settings, the information, like the previous settings, is no longer there.

A second-level sort is like a tie breaker. For example, names in the telephone book are sorted alphabetically by last name. Duplicate last names are sorted again by first name. Duplicate first names are sorted a third time by address.

Extracting data from a worksheet is like finding a telephone number in the telephone book and then writing it on a piece of paper. You locate the information that you want and place it in a separate area.

Defining a single row as an extract range is like bulldozing a lot. If your instructions are to bulldoze a lot, without specifics as to which part of the lot, you might bulldoze the entire lot.

A range is like a deck of cards with a rubber band around it. Just as you can add a card to the deck if you place the card inside the rubber band, you can insert a new row in a range if you place the new row within the end points of the range. And just as you cannot add a card to the deck if you place it outside the rubber band, you cannot insert a new row to the range if you place it outside the end points of the range.

Copying data is like making paper copies. Just as the original paper master remains intact when you copy papers, the cell contents remain intact when you copy data.

An empty cell in the criteria range is like an area without a gate keeper. The criterion you place in a cell becomes the gate keeper for that cell; it controls the flow of data through the cell. Because empty cells in the criteria range have no gate keeper, all data can flow through.

A Lotus setting sheet is like a scoreboard at a football game. Just as you look at the scoreboard when you want to check the scores, you look at the setting sheet when you want to check the current settings. You don't view either one continuously.

Word processing

The [CAPS LOCK] key is like a light switch. The same button turns it on and off.

The scroll bar is like an elevator shaft. Just as you use an elevator to move to different levels of a building, you use the scroll bar to move through a document.

The Clipboard is like a dumbwaiter. Just as the dumbwaiter transports food from one floor to another, the Clipboard transports information from one place to another.

Moving through a document is like scrolling a piece of paper. Only a portion of the document or paper is displayed at any given time. In both cases, the entire document is available and can be accessed by scrolling, or rolling the paper.

Page breaks are like busy intersections. Just as you have to brake when you come to a busy intersection, you have to use a break when you fill up a page.

An abort message is like a hurricane. Just as you don't get much warning of a hurricane, you don't know an abort message is coming until it's too late.

Buttons are like doorbells. Just as a doorbell completes a task when you press it, a button completes a task when you click on it.

The Move command is like taking furniture from one room to another; the Copy command is like getting another set of furniture for another room.

Moving text is like cutting and pasting paper objects. Just as you use scissors and paste to cut and move text on a sheet of paper, you use the Edit, Cut and Edit, Paste commands to move text in a document.

A style is like a recipe. A recipe contains instructions and a list of ingredients to create a specific food product, such as Chicken Kiev. Similarly, styles contain instructions and a list of attributes for a particular set of results. Each time you use a specific style, the same attributes are applied.

A style sheet is like a cookbook. Just as the cookbook contains a collection of recipes, the style sheet contains a collection of styles.

Templates are like stencils. Both contain forms that are already designed. Just as you add color to a stencil, you add text to a template.

A glossary is like a library. Both contain a collection of information that you can use repeatedly.

Using mail merge is like planning a class reunion. One person manages the class list (data source) and another person writes the letter (main document) announcing the reunion. Merging the two documents produces a personalized letter for each person in the class.

A text box is like a self-stick note. You use a text box to display a comment or reminder just as you use a self-stick note. You cannot see what is underneath a text box or a self-stick note without moving it.

Default tab stops are like stop signs. Just as you stop at each stop sign when you drive a car, you stop at each default tab stop when you press the [TAB] key.

References

Boothman, Terry. *The Media-Enhanced Classroom: Perspectives and Propositions*. Rochester, New York: Logical Operations, 1995.

Donaldson, Les and Edward E. Scannell. *Human Resource Development: The New Trainer's Guide*. Reading, Massachusetts: Addison-Wesley Publishing Company, Inc., 1986.

Kirkpatrick, Donald L. *Evaluating Training Programs: The Four Levels*. San Francisco, California: Barrett-Koehler Publishers, 1994.

Mager, Robert F. *Preparing Instructional Objectives*. Revised 2nd Ed. Belmont, California: Lake Publishing Company, 1984.

Masie, Elliot and Rebekah Wolman. *The Computer Training Handbook*. Raquette Lake, New York: National Training & Computers Project, 1988.

McGee-Cooper, Ann, with Duane Trammell and Barbara Lau. *You Don't Have To Go Home From Work Exhausted!* New York, New York: Bantom Books, 1992.

Mosher, Bob, Julie Nichols, Elliott Masie, Jeanie Maxfield, Renee Seibel, Terry Boothman, and Simone Banks. *How to Teach People to Use Computers*. Rochester, New York: Logical Operations, 1994.

Renner, Peter. *The Art of Teaching Adults: How to Become An Exceptional Instructor and Facilitator*. Vancouver, Canada: Training Associates, 1993.

Robinson, Russell D. *An Introduction to Helping Adults Learn and Change.* Milwaukee, Wisconsin: University of Wisconsin, 1987.

Silberman, Mel, assisted by Carol Auerbach. *Active Training: A Handbook of Techniques, Designs, Case Examples, and Tips.* San Diego, California: University Associates, 1990.